ITIL® Foundation Handbook

*it*SMF International
The IT Service Management Forum

London: T

information & publishing solutions

Published by TSO (The Stationery Office)
and available from:

Online
www.tsoshop.co.uk

Mail, Telephone, Fax & E-mail
TSO
PO Box 29, Norwich, NR3 1GN
Telephone orders/General enquiries:
0870 600 5522
Fax orders: 0870 600 5533
E-mail: customer.services@tso.co.uk
Textphone 0870 240 3701

TSO@Blackwell and other Accredited Agents

The AXELOS logo is a trade mark of AXELOS
Limited

The AXELOS swirl logo is a trade mark of
AXELOS Limited

ITIL® is a registered trade mark of AXELOS
Limited

PRINCE2® is a registered trade mark of AXELOS
Limited

MSP® is a registered trade mark of AXELOS
Limited

M_o_R® is a registered trade mark of AXELOS
Limited

MoP® is a registered trade mark of AXELOS
Limited

MoV® is a registered trade mark of AXELOS
Limited

P3O® is a registered trade mark of AXELOS
Limited

P3M3® is a registered trade mark of AXELOS
Limited

The Best Management Practice Official
Publisher logo is a trade mark of AXELOS
Limited

A CIP catalogue record for this book is available
from the British Library

A Library of Congress CIP catalogue record has
been applied for

First edition 2008
Second edition 2009
Third edition 2012

First published 2012
Third impression 2015

ISBN 9780113313495 Single copy ISBN
ISBN 9780113313501 (Sold in a pack of 10 copies)

Printed in the United Kingdom for
The Stationery Office

Material is FSC certified. Sourced from fully
sustainable forests.

P002495843   c308   08/12

Contents

Acknowledgements

AUTHORS

Claire Agutter, IT Training Zone Ltd

Alison Cartlidge, Steria

Ashley Hanna, HP

Stuart Rance, HP

Colin Rudd, itEMS Ltd

John A Sowerby, DPDHL IT Services

John Windebank, Oracle Corporation

REVIEWERS

Jeff Burns, independent consultant, Australia

Kate Cribb, Oakton Services, Australia

Carlos Fernandez-Baladron, independent consultant, Australia

Rosemary Gurney, Global Knowledge, UK

Jaqi Haworth, HDAA, Australia

Marcus Inglez, Technofor Iberica, Spain

Kirill Ivanov, INLINE Technologies, Russia

Roelof van der Kamp, ERKA Training & Promotion, The Netherlands

Ben Kalland, Tieturi, Finland

Dane Krstevski, National Bank of the Republic of Macedonia, Macedonia

Steve Mann, Opsys-sm2, Belgium

Reiko Morita, Ability InterBusiness Solutions, Japan

Rene Posthumus, BT Professional Services, The Netherlands

Liesbeth Riekwel, KPN Consulting, The Netherlands

Daniel Rodríguez Mañé, Government of Catalonia, Spain

Isao Tomita, ITpreneurs, Japan

Roger Tournois, KPN Corporate Market, The Netherlands

EDITORS

Alison Cartlidge, Steria

Mark Lillycrop, *it*SMF UK

About this guide

This guide provides a quick reference to the ITIL® framework for best practice in IT service management. It is designed as a study aid for students taking ITIL Foundation qualifications and as a handy portable reference source for managers, practitioners, vendors and consultants, in the workplace and on the move.

This guide is not intended to replace the more detailed ITIL publications or to be a substitute for a course provider's training materials.

USING THIS GUIDE TO OBTAIN THE ITIL FOUNDATION CERTIFICATE IN IT SERVICE MANAGEMENT

The content of this guide includes the learning experiences required by version 5.3 of the Foundation qualification syllabus (available for download at https://www.axelos.com/itil-qualifications). The guide also provides additional material for students and others who want a balanced level of understanding across the whole of ITIL. References to the ITIL V3 core publications are provided with the relevant section headings.

To help students studying for the Foundation qualification, the headings in this guide are identified with one of the following symbols to indicate whether the knowledge they contain should be studied.

Specific terminology required by the syllabus is defined the first time it is used.

Table 0.1 provides an alphabetical list of the ITIL service
management processes with cross-references to the publication
in which they are primarily defined, and to where significant
further expansion is provided. Most processes play a role during
each lifecycle stage, but only significant references are included.

Symbol	Significance
✔	The syllabus requires knowledge of this topic.
☑	This is a key process or function that should be learned in more detail and for which there may be more questions in the exam.
✘	This is material that may be of interest to the reader but is not required for the exam.

Table 0.1 ITIL service management processes and functions

Service management process	Syllabus	Primary source	Further expansion
Access management	✔	SO	
Availability management	✔	SD	SS, CSI
Business relationship management	✔	SS	SD, CSI
Capacity management	✔	SD	SO, CSI
Change evaluation	✘	ST	
Change management	☑	ST	
Demand management	✘	SS	SD
Design coordination	✔	SD	
Event management	✔	SO	

Table continues

Table 0.1 *continued*

Service management process	Syllabus	Primary source	Further expansion
Financial management for IT services	✔	SS	
Incident management	☑	SO	SD, CSI
Information security management	✔	SD	SO
IT service continuity management	✔	SD	
Knowledge management	✔	ST	CSI
Problem management	☑	SO	
Release and deployment management	✔	ST	
Request fulfilment	✔	SO	
Service asset and configuration management	✔	ST	
Service catalogue management	✔	SD	SS
Service level management	☑	SD	SS, CSI
Service portfolio management	✔	SS	SD
Service validation and testing	✘	ST	
Seven-step improvement process	✔	CSI	
Strategy management for IT services	✘	SS	
Supplier management	✔	SD	
Transition planning and support	✔	ST	SS

Service management process	Syllabus	Primary source	Further expansion
Service management function			
Application management	✔	SO	
IT operations management	✔	SO	
Service desk	☑	SO	
Technical management	✔	SO	

CSI *ITIL Continual Service Improvement;* SD *ITIL Service Design;* SO *ITIL Service Operation;* SS *ITIL Service Strategy;* ST *ITIL Service Transition.*

For the processes marked ✘, *knowledge of some of their concepts is still required for the Foundation exam. These are marked* ✔ *within the relevant chapters.*

1   Introduction

This quick reference guide describes the key principles and practices of IT service management (ITSM) as a set of resources and capabilities such as processes, people and technology as described by the ITIL service management framework.

1.1   BEST PRACTICE (SS 2.1.7) ✔

Organizations operating in dynamic environments need to improve their performance and maintain competitive advantage. Adopting best practices in industry-wide use can help to improve capability.

There are several sources for best practice:

- **Public frameworks and standards** These have been validated across diverse environments; knowledge is widely distributed among professionals; there is publicly available training and certification; acquisition of knowledge through the labour market is easier, as is collaboration and coordination across organizations.
- **Proprietary knowledge of organizations and individuals** This is customized for the local context and specific business needs; may only be available under commercial terms; may be tacit knowledge (inextricable and poorly documented).

1.2   THE ITIL FRAMEWORK (SS 1.2, 1.4) ✔

The ITIL framework is a source of best practice in service management. It is:

- Vendor-neutral
- Non-prescriptive
- Best practice.

ITIL is successful because it describes practices that enable organizations to deliver benefits, return on investment and sustained success, enabling organizations to:

- Deliver value for customers through services, improving customer relationships
- Integrate the strategy for services with the business strategy and customer needs
- Measure, monitor and optimize IT services and service provider performance and reduce costs
- Manage the IT investment and budget, risks, knowledge, capabilities and resources to deliver services effectively and efficiently
- Enable adoption of a standard approach to service management across the enterprise
- Change the organizational culture to support the achievement of sustained success.

ITIL guidance can be found in the following:

- **ITIL core** Best-practice publications applicable to all types of organizations that provide services to a business
- **ITIL complementary guidance** A complementary set of publications with guidance specific to industry sectors, organization types, operating models and technology architectures.

ITIL guidance can be adapted to support various business environments and organizational strategies. Complementary ITIL publications provide flexibility to implement the core in a diverse range of environments.

ITIL has been deployed successfully around the world for more than 20 years. Over this time, the framework has evolved from a specialized set of service management topics with a focus on function, to a process-based framework which now provides a broader holistic service lifecycle.

> **Definition: service lifecycle** ✔
>
> An approach to IT service management that emphasizes the importance of coordination and control across the various functions, processes and systems necessary to manage the full lifecycle of IT services. The service lifecycle approach considers the strategy, design, transition, operation and continual improvement of IT services. Also known as service management lifecycle.

The service lifecycle is described in a set of five publications within the ITIL core set. Each of these publications covers a stage of the service lifecycle (see Figure 1.1) from the initial definition and analysis of business requirements in *ITIL Service Strategy* (SS) and *ITIL Service Design* (SD), through migration into the live environment within *ITIL Service Transition* (ST), to live operation and improvement in *ITIL Service Operation* (SO) and *ITIL Continual Service Improvement* (CSI).

Figure 1.1 The ITIL service lifecycle

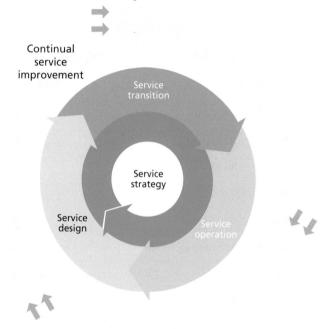

1.3   SERVICE MANAGEMENT (SS 2.1.1, 2.1.2, 2.1.3) ✔

To understand what service management is, we need to understand what services are, and how service management can help service providers to deliver and manage these services.

Definition: service ✔

A means of delivering value to customers by facilitating outcomes customers want to achieve without the ownership of specific costs and risks. The term 'service' is sometimes used as a synonym for core service, IT service or service package.

Definition: IT service ✔

A service provided by an IT service provider. An IT service is made up of a combination of information technology, people and processes. A customer-facing IT service directly supports the business processes of one or more customers and its service level targets should be defined in a service level agreement. Other IT services, called supporting services, are not directly used by the business but are required by the service provider to deliver customer-facing services.

The outcomes that customers want to achieve are the reason why they purchase or use a service. The value of the service to the customer is directly dependent on how well a service facilitates these outcomes.

Definition: outcome ✔

The result of carrying out an activity, following a process, or delivering an IT service etc. The term is used to refer to intended results as well as to actual results.

Services facilitate outcomes by enhancing the performance of associated tasks and reducing the effect of constraints. These constraints may include regulation, lack of funding or capacity, or technology limitations. The end result is an increase in the probability of desired outcomes. While some services enhance performance of tasks, others have a more direct impact – performing the task itself. Services can be classified as:

■ **Core services** Deliver the basic outcomes desired by one or more customers
■ **Enabling services** Needed for a core service to be delivered
■ **Enhancing services** Added to core services to make them more appealing to the customer.

Service management enables a service provider to:

■ Understand the services they are providing
■ Ensure that the services really do facilitate the outcomes their customers want to achieve
■ Understand the value of the services to their customers
■ Understand and manage all of the costs and risks associated with those services.

Definition: service management ✔

A set of specialized organizational capabilities for providing value to customers in the form of services.

These 'specialized organizational capabilities' are described in this guide. They include the processes, activities, functions and roles that service providers use to enable them to deliver services to their customers, as well as the ability to organize, manage knowledge, and understand how to facilitate outcomes that create value. However, service management is more than just a set of capabilities. It is also a professional practice supported by an extensive body of knowledge, experience and skills, with formal schemes for the education, training and certification of practising organizations.

Service management is concerned with more than just delivering services. Each service, process or infrastructure component has a lifecycle, and service management considers the entire lifecycle from strategy through design and transition to operation and continual improvement.

Every IT organization should act as a service provider, using the principles of service management to ensure that they deliver the outcomes required by their customers.

> **Definition: IT service management (ITSM)** ✔
>
> The implementation and management of quality IT services that meet the needs of the business. IT service management is performed by IT service providers through an appropriate mix of people, process and information technology.

1.4 PROCESSES AND FUNCTIONS
(SS 2.2.2, 2.2.3.1) ✔

> **Definition: process** ✔
>
> A process is a structured set of activities designed to accomplish a specific objective. A process takes one or more defined inputs and turns them into defined outputs. It may include any of the roles, responsibilities, tools and management controls required to reliably deliver the outputs. A process may define policies, standards, guidelines, activities and work instructions if they are needed.

Processes define actions, dependencies and sequence. Processes have the following characteristics:

- **Measurability** Processes can be measured and performance-driven, in management terms such as cost and quality, and in practitioner terms such as duration and productivity
- **Specific results** Processes exist to deliver a specific result that is identifiable and countable
- **Customers** Processes deliver their primary results to a customer or stakeholder, either internal or external, to meet their expectations
- **Responsiveness to specific triggers** Processes may be ongoing or iterative, but should be traceable to a specific trigger.

The key outputs from any process are driven by the objectives and include process measurement, reports and improvement. Process outputs have to conform to operational norms derived from business objectives for the process to be effective. Process activities have to be undertaken with the minimum resources for the process to be efficient. Figure 1.2 illustrates a process model.

Figure 1.2 Process model

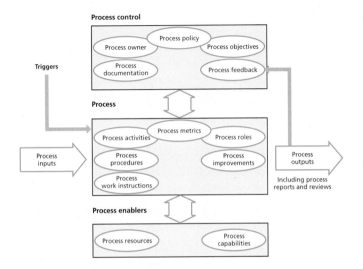

An organization needs to clearly define the roles and responsibilities required to undertake the processes and activities involved in each lifecycle stage. These roles are assigned to individuals within an organization structure of teams, groups or functions.

Definition: function ✔

A team or group of people and the tools or other resources they use to carry out one or more processes or activities – for example, the service desk.

Functions are self-contained with capabilities and resources necessary for their performance and outcomes. They provide structure and stability to organizations. Coordination between functions through shared processes is a common organizational design.

ITIL Service Operation describes the service desk, technical management, IT operations management and application management functions in detail, with technical and application management providing the technical resources and expertise to manage the whole service lifecycle.

1.5   ROLES ✔

A role is a set of responsibilities, activities and authorities granted to a person or team. A role is defined in a process or function. One person or team may have multiple roles. ITIL does not describe all the roles that could possibly exist in an organization, but provides representative examples to aid in an organization's definition of their own roles.

Roles fall into two main categories – generic roles (e.g. process owner) and specific roles that are involved within a particular lifecycle stage or process. Generic roles are described below, whilst specific roles are covered in the relevant lifecycle chapters of the core ITIL publications.

Note that service manager is a generic term for any manager within the service provider. The term is commonly used to refer to a business relationship manager, a process manager or a senior manager with responsibility for IT services overall. A service manager is often assigned several roles such as business relationship management, service level management and continual service improvement (CSI).

1.5.1   Process owner (SD 6.3.2) ✔

The process owner role is accountable for ensuring that a process is fit for purpose, i.e. that it is capable of meeting its objectives; that it is performed according to the agreed and documented standard; and that it meets the aims of the process definition. This role may be assigned to the same person carrying out the process manager role.

Key accountabilities include:

- Sponsoring, designing and change managing the process and its metrics
- Defining the process strategy, with periodic reviews to keep current, and assisting with process design
- Defining appropriate policies and standards for the process, with periodic auditing to ensure compliance
- Communicating process information or changes as appropriate to ensure awareness
- Providing process resources to support activities required throughout the service lifecycle
- Ensuring that process technicians understand their role and have the required knowledge to deliver the process
- Addressing issues with the running of the process
- Identifying enhancement and improvement opportunities and making improvements to the process.

1.5.2   Process manager (SD 6.3.3) ✔

The process manager role is accountable for operational management of a process. There may be several process managers for one process, for example for different locations. The process manager role is often assigned to the same person carrying out the process owner role.

Key accountabilities include:

- Working with the process owner to plan and coordinate all process activities
- Ensuring that all activities are carried out as required throughout the service lifecycle
- Appointing people to the required roles and managing assigned resources
- Working with service owners and other process managers to ensure the smooth running of services
- Monitoring and reporting on process performance
- Identifying opportunities for and making improvements to the process.

1.5.3 Process practitioner (SD 6.3.4) ✔

A process practitioner is responsible for carrying out one or more process activities. The process practitioner role may be combined with the process manager role, if appropriate.

Responsibilities typically include:

- Carrying out one or more activities of a process
- Understanding how their role contributes to the overall delivery of service and creation of value for the business
- Working with other stakeholders, such as their manager, co-workers, users and customers, to ensure that their contributions are effective
- Ensuring that inputs, outputs and interfaces for their activities are correct
- Creating or updating records to show that activities have been carried out correctly.

1.5.4   Service owner (SD 6.3.1) ✔

The service owner is responsible to the customer for the initiation, transition and ongoing maintenance and support of a particular service and accountable to the IT director or service management director for the delivery of a specific IT service. The service owner's accountability for a specific service within an organization is independent of where the underpinning technology components, processes or professional capabilities reside.

Service ownership is critical to service management and a single person may fulfil the service owner role for more than one service. Key responsibilities include:

- Ensuring that the ongoing service delivery and support meet agreed customer requirements via effective service monitoring and performance
- Working with business relationship management to ensure that the service provider can meet customer requirements
- Ensuring consistent and appropriate communication with customer(s) for service-related enquiries and issues
- Representing the service across the organization, including in change advisory board (CAB) meetings
- Serving as the point of escalation (notification) for major incidents relating to the service
- Participating in internal and external service review meetings
- Participating in negotiating service level agreements (SLAs) and operational level agreements (OLAs) relating to the service
- Identifying opportunities for and making improvements to the service.

The service owner is responsible for continual improvement and the management of change affecting the service under their care. The service owner is a primary stakeholder in all of the underlying IT processes which enable or support the service they own.

1.5.5   The RACI model (SD 3.7.4.1) ✔

Roles are accountable or responsible for an activity. However, as services, processes and their component activities run through an entire organization, each activity must be clearly mapped to well-defined roles. To support this, the RACI model or 'authority matrix' can be used to define the roles and responsibilities in relation to processes and activities.

RACI is an acronym for:

- **Responsible** The person or people responsible for correct execution – for getting the job done
- **Accountable** The person who has ownership of quality and the end result. Only one person can be accountable for each task
- **Consulted** The people who are consulted and whose opinions are sought. They have involvement through input of knowledge and information
- **Informed** The people who are kept up to date on progress. They receive information about process execution and quality.

Only one person should be accountable for any process or individual activity, although several people may be responsible for executing parts of the activity.

2 Service strategy

Successful organizations tend to have a clear set of overall objectives, and a clear business strategy associated with those objectives. A business strategy explains how an organization intends to achieve its objectives over time, underpinned by a series of individual strategies for each unit of that organization, one of which is an IT strategy. Business strategy therefore defines the IT strategy, and the IT strategy supports and validates business strategy.

An IT strategy typically covers multiple aspects, including the IT technology strategy and the IT service strategy. The IT service strategy explains how IT services will be used to enable IT to achieve its objectives, and how IT services underpin the overall business strategy.

ITIL Service Strategy focuses on the concepts an IT service provider can use to build its IT service strategy. A successful IT service strategy sets clear objectives and performance expectations for the IT service provider as it serves its targeted customers.

2.1 PURPOSE, OBJECTIVES, SCOPE AND VALUE OF SERVICE STRATEGY

2.1.1 Purpose and objectives (SS 1.1.1) ✔

The purpose of the service strategy stage in the ITIL service lifecycle is to define the perspective, position, plans and patterns that a service provider needs to consider in order to be able to meet its organization's desired business objectives (the four Ps of service strategy – see section 2.3.4).

A service strategy must identify:

- How the service provider intends to become, and remain, uniquely valuable to its customers
- The service provider's intended unique approach to creating and delivering value to its customers
- Its objectives in terms of the business outcomes it intends to enable
- The constraints the service provider must work within, including the competitive alternatives within which the service provider operates.

The objectives of the service strategy stage of the ITIL lifecycle include providing the service provider with:

- An understanding of what strategy is
- The necessary processes to:
  - Define its service strategy
  - Identify which services it needs to provide to achieve its strategy
  - Predict what levels of service demand it should expect as a result of its strategy
  - Determine what level of investment is required to achieve its strategy
  - Enable a working relationship between the service provider and its customers
- A clear definition of its services and the customers that use them
- A clear articulation of how services will be created, delivered and funded, who they will be delivered to and how each service delivers value
- Understanding of the organizational capability required to deliver the service strategy
- Clarity on which of its service assets are used to deliver each service and how the performance of these service assets can be optimized.

2.1.2   Scope (SS 1.1.2) ✔

ITIL Service Strategy is intended for use by both internal and external service providers.

Two aspects of strategy are covered in *ITIL Service Strategy*:

- ■ Defining a strategy whereby a service provider will deliver services to meet a customer's business outcomes
- ■ Defining a strategy for how to manage those services.

2.1.3   Value to business (SS 1.1.4) ✔

Any investment by a service provider in service strategy must deliver business value in return. The typical benefits gained from adopting and implementing service strategy best practice include:

- ■ A greater ability to understand and articulate the links between the service provider's IT service assets, its activities and the critical outcomes its customers achieve as a result of using its services
- ■ The service provider being seen by its organization and its customers to be contributing to value, not just to cost
- ■ A more flexible and timely ability to adapt its IT services to pre-empt and meet changing business needs – ensuring increased competitive advantage over time
- ■ A maintained portfolio of qualified services
- ■ Improved use of IT investments, where service development investment is driven by business priorities and clear return on investment (ROI) analysis.

2.2   KEY PRINCIPLES

2.2.1   Utility and warranty (SS 2.1.6) ✔

Customer perception of value from an IT service is influenced by the combination of two aspects of that service: its utility (its fitness for purpose) and its warranty (its fitness for use).

The value of an IT service to a customer is formed from the combination of that service's utility and warranty. Both utility and warranty must exist for an IT service to provide value to the customer, because customers cannot derive benefit from something that is fit for purpose but not fit for use (or vice versa).

> **Definition: utility** ✔
>
> Utility is the functionality offered by a product or service to meet a particular need. Utility can be summarized as 'what the service does', and can be used to determine whether a service is able to meet its required outcomes, or is 'fit for purpose'. The business value of an IT service is created by the combination of utility and warranty.

Definition: warranty ✔

Warranty is the assurance that a product or service will meet agreed requirements. This may be a formal agreement such as a service level agreement or contract, or it may be a marketing message or brand image. Warranty refers to the ability of a service to be available when needed, to provide the required capacity, and to provide the required reliability in terms of continuity and security. Warranty can be summarized as 'how the service is delivered', and can be used to determine whether a service is 'fit for use'. The business value of an IT service is created by the combination of utility and warranty.

2.2.2 Value creation through services ✔

A physical product generally has some form of intrinsic value – its resale value. But the value of a service comes from what it enables someone to do, not from what the service is made from. Therefore, the value of a service is not determined by the service provider, but by the customer – whoever receives that service (see section 2.2.10 for further explanation of 'customer'). The customer is uniquely positioned to understand what type of return they will achieve by using the service. Customers value an IT service when they see a clear relationship between the service and the business objectives they need to achieve.

2.2.2.1 Characteristics of value (SS 3.2.3) ✔

The value of a service can be characterized in the following terms:

- **Value is defined by the customer** Irrespective of a service provider's suggested value for their service, it is the customer that ultimately decides whether or not they perceive a service to be sufficiently valuable to them.

■ **Affordable mix of features** Customers make choices from the various services available to them based upon which service offering has the most effective mix of features at a price they are willing to pay.

■ **Achievement of objectives** Customers perceive most value from those services that they can associate with their business objectives. This value might not necessarily be measured in pure financial objectives.

■ **Value changes over time and circumstance** A customer's perception of what is valuable to them is likely to differ over time, as their business priorities change.

Bearing in mind these characteristics, the perceived value of an IT service provider is influenced by three core questions:

■ What IT services are being provided to the customer?
■ What is the customer achieving as a result of using the IT services?
■ What is the cost of the IT services to the customer?

2.2.2.2 Creating value (SS 3.2.3.1) ✓

It can be relatively simple to quantify the financial value of a service if it can be directly related to business outcomes that are also measured in financial terms. However, it is more difficult to evaluate the value of a service when related business outcomes are not directly linked to a monetary value.

There are additional factors that influence customer perception of value, in addition to just the ability of the service to enable the customer to achieve business outcomes. These additional contributory factors are the customer's preferences and the customer's perceptions (see Figure 2.1).

Figure 2.1 Components of value

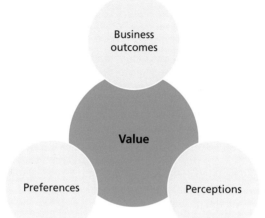

2.2.2.3 Perception of value (SS 3.2.3.1) ✔

A customer's perception of a service provider and of the value of the services from that service provider is influenced by:

- The attributes of the services delivered
- The customer's present and prior experience; of similar attributes, the supplier and the supplier's competitors and peers
- The relative capability of the service provider's competitors
- The customer's self-image and position in its market, i.e. does the customer position itself as an innovator or as a low-risk option?

Service providers need to understand, articulate and measure how effective their services are in enabling their customers to achieve their desired outcomes and consider any potential differences between what the customer perceives as valuable and what the service provider believes it provides.

Figure 2.2 illustrates how customers tend to perceive the economic value of a service. The starting point of the customer's perception is the customer's own reference value, based on the value from currently doing the activity themselves, from previous experience or from a similar service. The reference value may not necessarily be based on hard facts.

The positive difference of the proposed service is based on the additional benefits that the customer perceives they will gain, beyond any benefits in the reference value. These differences would be a combination of the additional utility and/or warranty offered within the proposed service.

The negative difference is the customer's perception of what they might lose if they took the proposed service.

The net difference is the customer's overall perception of how much better (or worse) the value proposition is from the proposed service compared to the reference value.

The economic value is the total value that the customer perceives the proposed service will deliver, including the reference value. This is the overall measure of the customer's perception of their ability to meet their desired outcomes when using the proposed service.

Figure 2.2 How customers perceive value

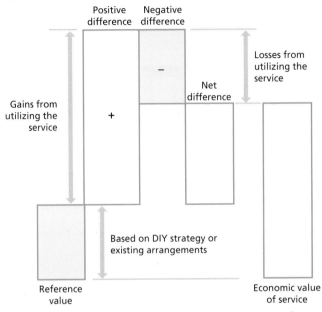

2.2.3 Assets, resources and capabilities (SS 2.2.1) ✔

An IT service provider has a set of assets that it uses to create IT services for its customers. Each of the service provider's customers uses those IT services to enable its own (customer) assets to generate business value. The service relationship between the service provider and the customer involves an interaction of the assets of each party.

Figure 2.3 The interaction of service provider and customer assets

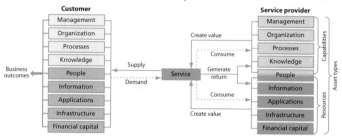

Figure 2.3 demonstrates how IT service providers utilize their service assets (in the form of resources and capabilities) to create each service that they provide, and how the service provider's customers use their own customer assets to create business outcomes from that service.

Definition: assets ✔

Asset: Any resource or capability. The assets of a service provider include anything that could contribute to the delivery of a service. Assets can be one of the following types: management, organization, process, knowledge, people, information, applications, infrastructure or financial capital.

Customer asset: Any resource or capability used by a customer to achieve a business outcome.

Service asset: Any resource or capability used by a service provider to deliver services to a customer.

Definition: resource ✔

This is a generic term that includes IT infrastructure, people, money or anything else that might help to deliver an IT service. Resources are considered to be assets of an organization.

Definition: capability ✔

The ability of an organization, person, process, application, IT service or other configuration item to carry out an activity. Capabilities are intangible assets of an organization.

The key difference between resource assets and capability assets is that distinctive capabilities can typically only be developed over time. Capabilities reflect experience and are used to transform resources into services. The distinctive capabilities of a service provider set it apart from its competitors, and enable it to attract and retain customers by offering unique value propositions.

Resources are the basic direct inputs to the production of a service, whereas capabilities represent the organization's ability to effectively coordinate, control and deploy its resources to produce value.

Resources are typically relatively easy to acquire, whereas capabilities reflect the organization's ability to embed its experience and knowledge into its people, processes and technologies.

Figure 2.4 demonstrates the relationships between business outcomes, customer assets, service assets, constraints and service management. An IT service provider utilizes its service management capabilities to optimize its service assets and minimize the impact of its inherent constraints. The customer uses IT services to optimize how it uses its own assets and reduce constraints within the customer organization. This, in turn, enables the customer to create the business outcomes it requires.

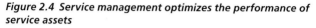

Figure 2.4 Service management optimizes the performance of service assets

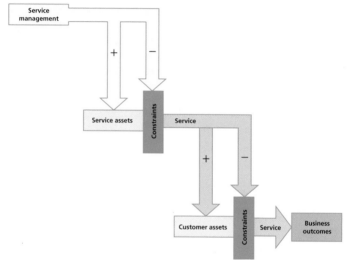

2.2.4 Patterns of business activity (SS 4.4.5.2) ✔

Figure 2.3 demonstrates that a customer's business activity generates demand for services. Business activity is performed by the customer's assets, and this activity tends to be performed in distinct patterns, these being known as 'patterns of business activity' (PBA).

It is important that service providers study each of their customers to identify, analyse and codify these patterns, because customer PBA will heavily influence what the service provider will see in the form of patterns of demand for its services. PBA definitions typically include:

- **Classification** An indication of the type of PBA, such as where the activity originates (user or automated), the type and impact of the outcomes, and the type of workload.
- **Attributes** The frequency, volume, location and duration of the activity.
- **Requirements** Aspects such as the performance, security, availability and tolerance for delays.
- **Service asset requirements** A utilization profile for the PBA, describing what assets it uses, when and in what quantity.

> **Definition: pattern of business activity** ✔
>
> A workload profile of one or more business activities. Patterns of business activity are used to help the IT service provider understand and plan for different levels of business activity.

2.2.5 Service portfolio (SS 4.2.4.1) ✔

The service portfolio describes services currently being considered and being developed by the service provider, along with its present contractual commitments, ongoing service improvement plans (SIPs), and retired services – those services that the service provider no longer provides. A service portfolio also includes any third-party services that are used by the service provider as an integral component of its service offerings to its customers.

A service portfolio portrays a service provider's commitments and investments across all of its customers and in all of the market spaces that the service provider operates or intends to operate in.

A service provider is heavily reliant upon its service portfolio when making decisions on which services to invest in and which to retire. The service portfolio enables the service provider to answer strategic questions such as:

- Why should a customer buy these services?
- Why should a customer buy these services from us?
- What are the pricing or chargeback models?
- What are the strengths and weaknesses, priorities and risks associated with each service?
- How should our resources and capabilities be allocated?

> **Definition: service portfolio** ✔
>
> The complete set of services that is managed by a service provider. The service portfolio is used to manage the entire lifecycle of all services, and includes three categories: service pipeline (proposed or in development), service catalogue (live or available for deployment), and retired services.

Service portfolio management is the governance of the service portfolio, and is described in section 2.3.1.

The components of the service portfolio are shown in Figure 2.5. These components are described in the relevant sections later in this publication.

Figure 2.5 The service portfolio

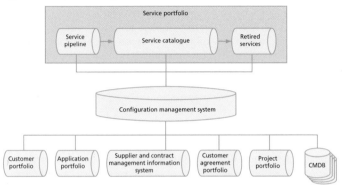

2.2.6 Governance (SS 2.3.1) ✔

Governance ensures that clear strategy is set and that suitable policies are defined and operated to enable that strategy to be achieved. It defines the overall common direction, policies and rules that both the business and IT use to conduct business.

The international standard for corporate governance of IT is ISO/IEC 38500.

> **Definition: governance** ✔
>
> Ensures that policies and strategy are actually implemented, and that required processes are correctly followed. Governance includes defining roles and responsibilities, measuring and reporting, and taking actions to resolve any issues identified.

2.2.7 Business case (SS 3.6.1.1) ✔

A business case is typically required whenever a major investment decision needs to be taken. It is a decision support and planning tool that explains the objectives of a proposed initiative and the specific business impacts (costs, risks and benefits) that the initiative is expected to generate. Business cases are used by a service provider when making decisions on whether requests for investment in service management initiatives should, or should not, be approved.

The contents of a business case vary from organization to organization, but all effective business cases contain detailed analysis of the potential business impacts. This generally includes some form of financial analysis of the consequence of a decision, typically in the form of an ROI analysis.

> **Definition: business case** ✔
>
> Justification for a significant item of expenditure. The business case includes information about costs, benefits, options, issues, risks and possible problems.

A business case for investment in a new service generally includes the following elements:

- **Introduction** Explanation of the business objectives addressed by the service
- **Business impacts** Identification of the expected financial and non-financial results from the new service
- **Risk and contingencies** Description of the risk of potential alternate results from those expected and identification of mitigation strategies to minimize or eliminate those risks

■ **Recommendations** Indication of the recommended decision-making actions.

2.2.8 Risk management (SS 5.6.5.1, 5.6.5.2) ✔

Risk management is relevant across the entire service lifecycle. *ITIL Service Strategy* covers the key aspects of risk management, and discusses risk management specifically in the context of IT service management (ITSM) implementation projects. Risk management frameworks that can be used to manage risk are detailed in section 8.3.

The responsibility for risk management within an ITSM implementation project falls with the project manager, although some ITSM implementation projects may be large enough for a specific individual in the project to be assigned to the role.

Risk management encompasses ensuring that risks are adequately identified, appropriate measures are put in place to mitigate against the risks, the risks are monitored and that the risk mitigation plan is reviewed at regular control points throughout the project.

Planning for risk management essentially involves:

■ **Identifying the risks** The task of initially identifying and naming potential threats to the success of the project.
■ **Analysing the risks** Once a list of potential risks has been compiled, the impact and probability of each risk can be assessed. The impact is the effect on the project if the risk becomes reality. This analysis describes the consequences (used to define how to deal with risks) and impacts along with some form of associated numeric value (used to rank the risks).

Once the project risks have been identified and analysed, a risk management plan is built to control and address these risks. The risks and the plan then need to be regularly reviewed to check that appropriate actions have taken place and have been successful.

A core principle of risk management is the recognition that project risks may become more or less probable over the duration of a project, and their potential impact may also change as the project progresses. Mechanisms for monitoring and controlling this potential for change must be built into the overall project management approach – every key project meeting should include a review of the risk management plan and an assessment of any new risks.

> **Definition: risk management** ✔
>
> The process responsible for identifying, assessing and controlling risks. Risk management is also sometimes used to refer to the second part of the overall process after risks have been identified and assessed, as in 'risk assessment and management'. This process is not described in detail within the core ITIL publications.

2.2.9 Service providers (SS 2.1.4) ✔

Every IT organization should act as a service provider, using service management to ensure they deliver the outcomes required by their customers.

To successfully execute against its service strategy, a service provider must achieve a real understanding of who its customers are, who its target customers should be and what business outcomes it wants to enable. This requires the service provider to take pause to consider their current and planned operating models, and to achieve a clear view of the type of service provider they are or what they may need to become.

> **Definition: service provider** ✓
>
> An organization supplying services to one or more internal customers or external customers. Service provider is often used as an abbreviation for IT service provider.

> **Definition: IT service provider** ✓
>
> A service provider that provides IT services to internal or external customers.

Service providers fall into three broad categories:

- ■ **Type I – internal service provider** Exists within a business unit solely to deliver IT services to that one specific business unit. There could be multiple Type I service providers in an organization.
- ■ **Type II – shared services unit** An internal service provider delivering IT services to multiple business units in the same organization.
- ■ **Type III – external service provider** Provides IT services to external customers.

Some aspects of service management apply differently to certain categories of service providers. Customers, contracts, competition, market spaces, revenue and strategy are examples of facets which might take on different meanings depending on the type of service provider involved.

In a large organization it is not unusual for IT services to be delivered through a combination of dedicated and shared internal service providers, along with external service providers delivering outsourced services.

2.2.10 Stakeholders in service management (SS 2.1.5) ✔

Service providers have many different internal stakeholders, including the functions, groups and teams that deliver the services. External stakeholders include:

- **Customers** Those who buy goods or services. For an IT service provider, this is the person or group who defines and agrees the service level targets.
- **Users** Those who use the service on a day-to-day basis, as distinct from a customer who may not use the IT service directly. Users may not necessarily be within the customer organization.
- **Suppliers** Third parties responsible for supplying goods or services required to deliver IT services.

The term 'customer' is sometimes used generically by a service provider to refer to anyone that receives a service of some kind. This is important in the approach to ensuring that IT staff demonstrate good customer service behaviour whenever they interact with individuals in a customer organization. However, it is also important that the service provider clearly recognizes and distinguishes between those who are true 'customers' of its services and those that are 'users' of its services.

2.2.11 Internal and external customers (SS 3.2.1.2) ✔

There is a difference between customers who work in the same organization as the IT service provider and customers who work for other organizations.

■ **Internal customers** People or departments who work for the
   same organization as the IT service provider.
■ **External customers** People who work for a different
   organization or organizations that are separate legal entities
   from the IT service provider and purchase services via a
   legally binding contract or agreement.

Both internal and external customers must be provided with the
agreed level of service, with the same levels of customer service.
However, the way that services are designed, transitioned,
delivered and improved is often different. Differences between
internal and external customers include:

■ Funding and accounting
■ Links to business strategy and objectives
■ Involvement in service design, transition and operation
■ Drivers for improvement.

2.2.12 Internal and external services (SS 3.2.2.3) ✔

There are differences between internal and external services;
internal services are delivered between departments within the
same organization, whereas external services are delivered to
customers outside of the service provider's overall organization
(see Figure 2.6).

Figure 2.6 Internal and external services

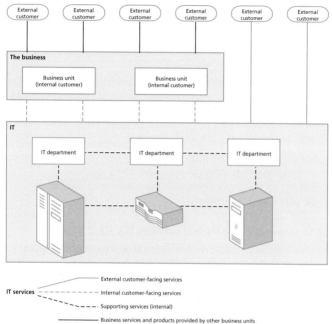

By classifying its services into 'supporting', 'internal' and 'external' categories, a service provider can differentiate between services that support an internal activity from services that actually achieve business outcomes for external customers:

- **Supporting services** Services not directly used by the business or external customers, enabling the IT processes and services used by the IT service provider to provide other services. The performance of supporting services is managed by OLAs.
- **Internal customer-facing services** Services directly supporting one or more business processes that are managed by an internal customer. These services are managed by SLAs and are underpinned by supporting services.
- **External customer-facing services** Services that are supplied directly from IT to external customers. These services are provided to enable the overall organization to meet certain strategic objectives, and as such, are business services in their own right. These services are managed through a contract.

2.2.13 Service model (SS 3.4.7) ✗

Definition: service model ✗

A model that shows how service assets interact with customer assets to create value. Service models describe the structure of a service (how the configuration items fit together) and the dynamics of the service (activities, flow of resources and interactions). A service model can be used as a template or blueprint for multiple services.

Service models can be in many forms, from simple diagrams showing the different components of a service and their dependencies and relationships, to complex analytical models that allow the dynamics of a service to be analysed under different configurations and demand patterns.

Service models can be used by a service provider to:

- Understand what it will take to deliver a new service

- Identify and map the assets that are involved in a service and the associated interfaces between technology, people and processes
- Illustrate how value is created by a service
- Assess the impact of change upon an existing service.

2.3 PROCESSES AND ACTIVITIES

2.3.1 Service portfolio management (SS 4.2) ✔

2.3.1.1 Purpose and objectives (SS 4.2.1) ✔

The purpose of service portfolio management is to ensure that a service provider has the right mix of services to meet its overall service strategy. Service portfolio management is more than the passive administration of a list of services; it is the governance process of the service portfolio – the process by which a service provider manages its investments across the service lifecycle, considering each service in terms of the business value it provides.

A service provider uses service portfolio management to control the entry of any service into the service portfolio, by tracking any investment in services through its lifecycle of development, delivery and retired stages. Service portfolio management ensures that the entry or exit of a service from any stage is dependent on the approval of funding, requiring an appropriate financial plan for recovering costs or generation of the desired level of profit (depending on the nature of the service provider's organization).

The objectives of service portfolio management include:

- Enabling a service provider to investigate and make decisions on which services to provide and which to retire, based on an analysis of the risk and potential return

- Management of a definitive portfolio of services, including a clear articulation of the business needs that each service addresses and the business outcomes it supports
- Evaluation of the degree to which each of its services enables the service provider to achieve its service strategy
- Control of which services are offered, under what conditions and at what level of investment
- To track each investment in service throughout the lifecycle of each service.

2.3.1.2   Scope (SS 4.2.2) ✔

The scope of service portfolio management encompasses:

- Services that are planned to be delivered
- Services that are currently being delivered
- Services that have been withdrawn from service (retired).

The core focus of service portfolio management is tracking the ongoing viability of each service, in terms of its ability to generate value and support the service provider to achieve its overall service strategy.

An internal service provider's execution of service portfolio management requires them to work closely with each business unit in the organization to assess service investment and returns.

External service providers tend to be able to evaluate the value of each service more overtly, as each service should either directly generate profit or support services that are profit generating.

2.3.1.3   Value to business (SS 4.2.3) ✘

Service portfolio management enables the business to make sound decisions on investment and de-investment in services, ensuring that such decisions are made on the basis of a robust business case.

2.3.1.4   Principles and basic concepts (SS 4.2.4) ✗

A core principle of service portfolio management is that it enables a service provider to understand:

- The services it provides
- The investments in those services
- The strategy and objectives of each service in terms of business value.

Through this understanding the service provider can control and manage decisions about its services throughout the service lifecycle, and ensure sound business logic and sequence is applied to investment decisions, i.e. investment in detailed service design is not approved until adequate understanding is reached upon precisely which services should be offered and why.

The key concept in service portfolio management is the service portfolio, which is described in section 2.2.5.

2.3.1.5   Process activities, methods and techniques (SS 4.2.5) ✗

Service portfolio management consists of four main phases of activity:

- **Define** Collection and validation of the inventory of all existing and proposed services including their business cases.
- **Analyse** Identification of what services are needed for the service provider to achieve its service strategy, how well the existing service portfolio meets these needs, and how to prioritize and balance supply and demand.
- **Approve** Every service in the service portfolio, along with its associated level of investment, needs to be approved. All changes to services in the service portfolio also need approval, including the retirement of services.

■ **Charter** A charter is required to authorize each project to build, enhance or retire a service. The charter documents the project's scope and terms of reference along with approval decisions relating to agreed changes to the service portfolio.

2.3.1.6   Triggers, inputs, outputs and interfaces (SS 4.2.6) ✗

Triggers

■ Changes to the service strategy
■ Request for a new service or change to existing service
■ Continual service improvement (CSI) initiatives
■ Feedback from design, build, transition, operations, service level management (SLM) or financial management teams.

Inputs

■ Strategic plans
■ Financial reports
■ Requests, suggestions and complaints from the business
■ Project updates for services in the charter stage.

Outputs

■ Service portfolio updates
■ Service charters authorizing creation of new or changed services
■ Reports on the investment and returns from services
■ Change proposals to change management
■ Identified strategic risks.

Interfaces

■ **Service catalogue management** Service portfolio management determines which services should be in the catalogue, service catalogue management performs the activities required for this to be done.
■ **Strategy management for IT services** Defines what type of services should be in the portfolio, investment objectives and market space targets.

- **Financial management for IT services** Provides the information and tools to enable service portfolio management to perform ROI calculations.
- **Demand management** Provides information about PBA.
- **Business relationship management** Keeps customers informed on the status of services and provide inputs from the customers.
- **SLM** Provides feedback on actual service performance.

2.3.1.7 Critical success factors and key performance indicators (SS 4.2.8) ✗

Table 2.1 Examples of critical success factors and key performance indicators for service portfolio management

Critical success factor	Key performance indicator
A formal process to investigate and decide which services to provide	Formal service portfolio management process exists
	Service portfolio management process is reviewed annually
A model to analyse ROI and acceptable level of risk for new services and changes to existing services	Initial investment in each service is documented along with associated risks
	Regular accounting reports show ongoing ROI in each service
A formal process to review whether services are enabling the organization to achieve its strategy	Service portfolio management reports regularly on the performance of each service
	Audit of consistency between the service strategy and the service portfolio

Table 2.1 includes some sample critical success factors (CSFs) for service portfolio management, followed by a small number of typical key performance indicators (KPIs) that support each CSF. Achievement against KPIs should be monitored and used to identify opportunities for improvement, which should be logged in the CSI register for evaluation and possible implementation.

2.3.1.8   Challenges and risks (SS 4.2.9) ✗

Challenges
- Lack of access to business information
- Absence of formal project management or change management
- Absence of project or customer portfolio
- Service portfolio focused only on the service provider's aspect of its services.

Risks
- Customer pressures lead to poorly informed decisions on which services to offer and invest in
- Services being offered that cannot be adequately measured.

2.3.2   Financial management for IT services (SS 3.6.1.1, 4.3.1, 4.3.2) ✔

2.3.2.1   Purpose and objectives (SS 4.3.1) ✔

The purpose of financial management for IT services can be summarized as:

- To secure the appropriate level of funding to design, develop and deliver the IT services required to support the service strategy
- To ensure that the IT service provider does not commit to services that it is unable to deliver

■ To identify the balance between service cost and quality, and supply and demand.

Objectives include:

■ Define and maintain a framework to:
  – Secure funding to manage the provision of services
  – Identify, manage and communicate the cost of providing services
  – Recover costs of service provision (and required profit, in the case of external service providers)
■ Evaluate the financial impact of new or changed strategies
■ Execute enterprise and IT service provider specific financial policies and practices
■ Account for the money spent in the development, delivery and support of services
■ Forecast the financial requirements for the service provider.

2.3.2.2 Scope (SS 4.3.2) ✔

Financial management for IT services is often owned by a specific dedicated department within the IT service provider, typically reporting directly either to the CIO or CFO. It has three core aspects, each of which generally has an annual planning cycle and a monthly operational monitoring and reporting cycle:

■ **Accounting** Mechanisms by which the IT service provider accounts to its overall organization for the way its money was spent.
■ **Budgeting** Predicting and controlling the service provider's income and expenditure. Achieved through periodic negotiation cycles in which budgets are typically set annually and actual financial performance against these budgets is reported monthly.
■ **Charging** How the IT service provider bills its customers for services supplied.

2.3.2.3   Value to business (SS 4.3.3) ✗

Financial management for IT services enables and enhances decision-making ability, making the service provider more agile and effective, whilst also ensuring financial compliance and robust control. Common questions facilitated by good financial management regimes include:

- Is the service strategy resulting in sufficient profitability and revenue?
- Which services are the most inefficient and why?
- Are services being consumed in the volumes expected in the budget?

Service providers invest in financial management to ensure that their business is conducted in a financially responsible manner – allowing the organization to operate legally and without threat of non-compliance penalties. This rigour also leads to greater accuracy in planning and forecasting and a clearer understanding of the true costs and value of each IT service.

2.3.2.4   Principles and basic concepts (SS 4.3.4) ✗

An organization's overall financial management policies and practices are applied in a tightly aligned manner across all of its departments. This often creates an additional level of financial management process that is specific to that department's governance requirements, whilst continuing to conform to the organization's overall financial management process. *ITIL Service Strategy* makes the following terminology distinctions in recognition of these multiple levels of financial process:

- **Financial management** This is the generic use of the term.
- **Enterprise financial management** Refers specifically to the organization's overall financial management process, as used by the 'corporate' financial department.
- **Financial management for IT services** Refers to the specific way in which the IT service provider has applied the process.

Funding

Funding is the sourcing and allocation of money for specific purposes, i.e. funding for the design, transition, operation and improvement of a new IT service. Funding can be **external** or **internal**, i.e. either coming from revenue received from selling IT services to external customers, or from other business units within the IT service provider's organization.

Financial management for IT services and value

Financial models and practices that enable the calculation of value.

Compliance

The ability to demonstrate that proper and consistent accounting methods and practices are employed by the service provider.

2.3.2.5 Process activities, methods and techniques (SS 4.3.5) ✗

Financial management for IT services includes accounting, budgeting and charging (ABC):

- **Accounting** The process that tracks income from IT services against actual costs of delivery, comparing actual costs with budgets and managing any variance. Accounting encompasses the following activities, methods and techniques:
  - Cost models
  - Cost centres and cost units
  - Cost types and cost elements
  - Cost classification

- – Analysis and reporting
- – Action plans
- ■ **Budgeting** The activity of predicting and controlling the spending of money, including:
  - – Analysis of previous budgets
  - – Assessment of plans
  - – Cost and income estimation
  - – Producing budget(s)
- ■ **Charging** This is optional for internal service providers, depending upon their organization's overall enterprise financial management policies. For external service providers there is no option – this is the means by which the service provider gains revenue and profit. Charging encompasses:
  - – Charging policies
  - – Chargeable items
  - – Pricing
  - – Billing.

2.3.2.6 Triggers, inputs, outputs and interfaces (SS 4.3.6) ✗

Triggers

- ■ Periodic reporting cycles
- ■ Audits
- ■ Requests for financial information from other service management processes
- ■ The introduction of charging for internal IT services, or the need to determine the price of an external service.

Inputs

- ■ Legal, regulatory and enterprise financial management policies, standards and practices
- ■ Generally accepted accounting practices (GAAP)
- ■ Data sources where financial information is stored (supplier database, configuration management system (CMS) etc.)

■ The service portfolio.

Outputs
■ Service valuation
■ Service investment analysis
■ Compliance
■ Cost optimization
■ Business impact analysis (BIA)
■ Planning confidence.

Interfaces
■ **All service management processes** Financial management for IT services is used in each process to determine the costs and benefits of that process.
■ **Strategy management for IT services** The translation of organizational strategy into service strategy.
■ **Service portfolio management** Provides the service structure used to define cost and charging models.
■ **Business relationship management** Provides input into financial management on how the business measures the value of IT services.
■ **Capacity and availability management** Provides service performance information.

2.3.2.7 Critical success factors and key performance indicators (SS 4.3.8) ✗

Table 2.2 includes some sample CSFs for financial management for IT services, followed by a small number of typical KPIs that support each CSF. Achievement against KPIs should be monitored and used to identify opportunities for improvement, which should be logged in the CSI register for evaluation and possible implementation.

Table 2.2 Examples of critical success factors and key performance indicators for financial management for IT services

Critical success factor	Key performance indicator
An enterprise-wide framework to identify, manage and communicate financial information on the costs and associated return from IT services	Established enterprise financial management standards, policies and charts of accounts
	Timely and accurate financial reports
Financial management for IT services is a key component of evaluating strategies	All strategies have robust ROI analyses
	Accurate financial forecasts
Funding is available to support the provision of services	Funding available to provide the agreed services
	Funding is made available for research and development of new services
Money spent on the creation, delivery and support of services can be accurately accounted for	Use of adequate accounting systems
	Regular reporting on the costs of services
The service provider is able to charge for services where appropriate	Charging is accurate, timely and conducted as agreed with customers
	Customer complaints and queries about charging are below the agreed percentage and are resolved within agreed timescales

2.3.2.8 Challenges and risks (SS 4.3.9) ✗

Challenges

- Financial reporting can be focused too heavily on the cost of infrastructure and applications rather than the total cost of services
- The chart of accounts for financial management for IT services needs to be appropriate and relevant to the needs of an IT service provider, not just conformant with the overall policies of enterprise financial management
- A focus on cost reduction rather than cost optimization
- Difficulties involved in introducing internal charging for IT services – this will require a change in culture, in the way in which IT service success is measured and in the way in which value is articulated.

Risks

- Making poorly informed investment decisions due to a lack of dedicated financial management for IT services resources
- Exposure to penalties for non-compliance to legislative and regulatory requirements
- Lack of access to suitably skilled and qualified staff that understand both the world of an IT service provider and the world of cost accounting.

2.3.3   Business relationship management (SS 4.5) ✔

2.3.3.1   Purpose and objectives (SS 4.5.1) ✔

Business relationship management is the process that enables business relationship managers (BRMs) to provide effective links between the service provider and its customers, so that the service provider can understand the business requirements of their customers and provide services that meet the needs of their customers. The success of the business relationship management process is primarily indicated by the measure of customer satisfaction within the service provider's customer base.

The purpose of the business relationship management process includes:

■ **Enabling effective business relationships** between the service provider and its customers.

■ **Identifying customer needs** and ensuring that the service provider continues to recognize and understand each customer and their individual business needs as they change over time.

■ **Assisting the customer to understand the value of the service(s)** provided and ensuring customer expectation does not exceed what they are willing to pay for.

■ **Ensuring that the service provider fully understands the customer requirement** and is able to meet the customer's expectations before agreeing to deliver the service.

Business relationship management objectives include enabling the service provider to:

■ Prioritize its services and service assets to meet their customers' perspective of service requirements

■ Sustain high levels of customer satisfaction

■ Establish and maintain constructive business relationships with its customers

■ Identify changes in its customers' environments and technology trends that could impact the services to individual customers

■ Establish and articulate its customers' business requirements for services

- Mediate in situations where there are conflicting requirements for services from different customers
- Establish formal complaints and escalation procedures for each of its customers.

2.3.3.2   Scope (SS 4.5.2) ✔

The scope of business relationship management for internal service providers focuses on the alignment of objectives of the various business units with the activities of the IT service provider. This typically involves interaction between a senior representative from IT and equivalent senior managers within each business unit. External service providers typically have a separate, dedicated, business relationship management function. Individuals in this group may be known as BRMs or account managers, and are typically assigned to one or more specific customers.

The business relationship management process focuses on understanding and communicating:

- Business outcomes that the customer wants to achieve
- Services currently provided to the customer
- How services are currently delivered
- Technology trends that may impact current services, and the nature of the potential impact upon each customer
- Customer satisfaction, and the status of any plans to address dissatisfaction
- How the service provider is represented to the customer.

There is potential for confusion between the business relationship management process and other key service management processes such as SLM. Business relationship management focuses on a more strategic level – to ensure the service provider is meeting the customer's overall needs, while SLM focuses on ensuring agreed levels of service are provided to the customer and users.

2.3.3.3 Value to business (SS 4.5.3) ✗

The value of business relationship management to the service provider's business includes:

- An ability to truly understand, articulate and meet the business needs of its customers
- Effective dialogue between the service provider and each of its customers, aligning the services provided with the customer's business needs
- Clearer understanding of the customer's business needs, and improved customer awareness of the service provider's capabilities
- A higher level of trust and collaboration between the customer and the service provider, enabling effective resolution of disagreements and more realistic customer expectations of the services provided.

2.3.3.4 Principles and basic concepts (SS 4.5.4) ✗

Business relationship manager (BRM)

The role of the BRM can be wider than the business relationship management process, with the BRM having a role in other service management processes, such as a BRM passing information on customer requirements into the service portfolio management process.

Customer portfolio

This is a record of all the service provider's customers. The prime purpose of the customer portfolio is to enable the service provider to quantify their commitments, investments and risks relative to each customer. Whilst the data is used by the service portfolio management process and several other service management processes, it is defined and maintained by the business relationship management process.

Customer agreement portfolio

A database or document used by the service provider to manage its service contracts with its customers. The customer agreement portfolio is actually managed under the SLM process, but is frequently used by a BRM.

Customer satisfaction

Business relationship management is responsible for ensuring that the service provider's customers are satisfied with the services they receive, that customer satisfaction is measured and assessed and any issues are addressed in a timely and effective manner.

Service requirements

Business relationship management is engaged in the definition and clarification of service requirements throughout the service lifecycle.

Business relationship management as facilitator of strategic partnerships

Business relationship management is the process that attempts to achieve the involvement of the service provider in the strategic discussions of their customers and the customer's willingness to contribute input and feedback into the service provider's strategic planning and service improvement activities.

2.3.3.5   Process activities, methods and techniques (SS 4.5.5) ✗

Business relationship management spans every stage in the service lifecycle, but it is rarely executed as a single, end-to-end process. Essentially, business relationship management involves two core activities:

- Representation of the service provider to its customers – through marketing, selling and delivery activities

■ Ensuring the service provider's responses to customer
requirements are appropriate – through work with service
portfolio management and design coordination.

2.3.3.6   Triggers, inputs, outputs and interfaces (SS 4.5.6) ✗

Triggers

■ New strategic initiatives
■ New or changed services
■ New opportunities
■ Customer requests
■ Customer complaints.

Inputs

■ Customer requirements
■ Customer requests, complaints, escalations or compliments
■ The service provider's service strategy
■ The customer's strategy
■ The service portfolio
■ SLAs
■ PBA and user profiles.

Outputs

■ Defined business outcomes
■ Agreement to fund (internal) or pay for (external) services
■ The customer portfolio
■ Service requirements for strategy, design and transition
■ Customer satisfaction survey results.

Interfaces
- **Strategy management for IT services** Identification of market spaces from information gathered from customers by business relationship management.
- **Service portfolio management** Customer requirements and environment information gathered by the BRM is essential in the creation of service models and in the assessment of proposed services for suitability.
- **Financial management for IT services** Input of customer financial objectives gathered by the BRM.
- **Demand management** Assistance provided by the BRM in the identification of patterns of business and user profiles, along with ongoing changes to these patterns and profiles.
- **SLM** Information provided by the BRM on customers' service requirements.

2.3.3.7 Critical success factors and key performance indicators (SS 4.5.8) ✗

Table 2.3 includes some sample CSFs for business relationship management, followed by a small number of typical KPIs that support each CSF. Achievement against KPIs should be monitored and used to identify opportunities for improvement, which should be logged in the CSI register for evaluation and possible implementation.

Table 2.3 Examples of critical success factors and key performance indicators for business relationship management

Critical success factor	Key performance indicator
Ability to document and understand customer requirements and desired business outcomes	Documented customer requirements and business outcomes
Ability to measure customer satisfaction levels, and to know what action to take with the results	Customer satisfaction feedback into service portfolio management
	Investigations into customer satisfaction when below an agreed minimum level
Ability to identify changes in the customer environment that could impact the type, level or utilization of services provided	Consistently high customer satisfaction and retention levels
	Provision of information from business relationship management that results in changes to services and strategy
Ability to establish and articulate business requirements for new or changed services	Documented requirements for new/changed services
	Reasons for, and expected results from, new/changed services are documented and signed off at the strategy, design and transition stages

Table continues

Table 2.3 *continued*

Critical success factor	Key performance indicator
Formal complaints and escalation processes are available to customers	Numbers of complaints and escalations are measured and trended
	Reduction in number of escalations

2.3.3.8   Challenges and risks (SS 4.5.9) ✗

Challenges

■ Business relationship management typically fails if it is introduced to purely work on levels of customer satisfaction. Business relationship management must take a more holistic approach that has influence in the definition of services and in the tracking that these services are delivered to the agreed levels

■ A lack of service provider credibility can make customers reluctant to invest their time in sharing requirements and feedback

■ Potential confusion between the role of the BRM and the process of business relationship management. BRMs execute activities from other processes in addition to business relationship management process activities, simply because of their unique position with the customer.

Risks

■ Potential for duplication of activities, and for activities being neglected due to confusion on the boundaries between the business relationship management process and other service management processes

■ The service provider can become ineffective if disconnects occur between customer facing processes (including business relationship management) and processes focusing more on technology (such as capacity management).

2.3.4   Strategy management for IT services (SS 4.1) ✗

2.3.4.1   Purpose and objectives (SS 4.1.1) ✗

Strategy management for IT services is the process of defining and maintaining an organization's perspective, position, plans and patterns (the four Ps of service strategy) with regard to its services and the management of those services.

The purpose of strategy management for IT services is to ensure that a service strategy is defined, maintained and managed to achieve its purpose.

The objectives of strategy management for IT services include:

■ A clearly articulated statement of the service provider's vision and mission, that is regularly reviewed (the service provider's **perspective**)

■ A definition of what services will be provided by the service provider, to what market spaces, and how competitive advantage will be maintained (the service provider's **position**)

■ Production, communication and maintenance of the service provider's strategic planning documents (the **plans**)

■ Definition of how the service provider will organize itself to enable the business objectives to be met – the service provider's **patterns**. A pattern of action is how an organization works.

2.3.4.2   Scope (SS 4.1.2) ✗

Strategy management is the responsibility of the executives of an organization, enabling them to set the objectives of the organization, to specify how the organization will meet those objectives and to prioritize investments required to meet them.

An organization's strategy is not limited to a single document or department. The overall strategy of an organization will be broken down into a strategy for each unit of the business. Strategy management for the enterprise has to ensure that these are all linked and consistent with one another. Strategy management for IT services has to ensure that the services and the way they are managed support the overall strategy of the enterprise.

The IT strategy (and therefore also the strategy for IT services) is derived from the business strategy, but it also provides validation of the business strategy. The IT strategy can determine whether a strategic objective is technologically possible, and what level of investment would be required to meet that objective. The business is then able to decide on whether the objective should be included and at what priority.

A service strategy is not the same as an ITSM strategy:

- **Service strategy** The strategy that a service provider will follow to define and execute services that meet a customer's business objectives. For an IT service provider the service strategy is a subset of the IT strategy.
- **Service management (ITSM) strategy** The plan for identifying, implementing and executing the processes used to manage services identified in a service strategy. In an IT service provider, the ITSM strategy will be a subset of the service strategy.

2.3.4.3 Value to business (SS 4.1.3)

The strategy of an organization defines its objectives; how it will meet those objectives; and how it will know it has met those objectives. Otherwise, an organization can only react to demands from stakeholders, with little ability to assess each demand and understand the impact to the organization.

A well-defined and managed strategy ensures that the resources and capabilities of the organization are aligned to achieving its business outcomes, and that investments match the organization's intended development and growth.

Strategy management ensures that:

- All stakeholders are represented in deciding the appropriate direction for the organization
- All stakeholders agree on organizational objectives and the means whereby resources, capabilities and investment are prioritized
- Resources, capabilities and investments are appropriately managed to achieve the strategy.

For a service provider, strategy management for IT services:

- Ensures an appropriate set of services in its service portfolio
- Ensures all services have a clear purpose, and everyone in the service provider organization knows their role in achieving that purpose
- Encourages appropriate levels of investment, leading to cost savings, increased levels of investment for key projects or service improvements and shifting investment priorities so that effort and budget are spent on the areas with the highest level of business impact.

For the customer of the service provider, strategy management for IT services enables them to articulate clearly their business priorities in a way that is understandable to the service provider.

2.3.4.4   Principles and basic concepts (SS 4.1.4) ✗
Strategy principles and concepts are defined in section 2.2.

2.3.4.5   Process activities, methods and techniques (SS 4.1.5) ✗
Key activities are:

- Strategic assessment
  - Analyse the internal environment: identify current strengths and weaknesses
  - Analyse the external environment: identify opportunities and threats, and how they will develop in the future
  - Define market spaces: define opportunities where a service provider can deliver value to its customer(s)
  - Identify strategic industry factors
  - Establish objectives
- Strategy generation, evaluation and selection (the four Ps of service strategy)
  - Determine perspective: defines overall direction, values, beliefs and purpose
  - Form a position: defines how the service provider will be differentiated from other service providers
  - Craft a plan: a strategic plan identifies how the organization will achieve its objectives, vision and position
  - Adopt patterns (ways of working): patterns that executives believe will be efficient and effective in achieving objectives, and a way of dealing with change, so that the strategy adapts and evolves along with the organization and its environment

- Strategy execution
  - Service management processes enable the service provider to achieve alignment between the services and the desired outcomes on an ongoing basis
  - Align assets with customer outcomes
  - Optimize CSFs
  - Prioritize investments
- Measurement and evaluation
  - CSI activities measure and evaluate the achievement of strategy over time
- Expansion and growth: once the organization becomes successful through its strategy, it is better able to deliver services to its existing market spaces and so expand into new customers or services.

The above applies equally to internal and external service providers.

2.3.4.6 Triggers, inputs, outputs and interfaces (SS 4.1.6) ✗

Triggers
- Annual planning cycles
- New business opportunity
- Changes to internal or external environments
- Mergers or acquisitions.

Inputs
- Existing plans
- Research on aspects of the environment
- Vendor strategies and product roadmaps
- Customer interviews and strategic plans
- Service portfolio
- Service reporting
- Audit reports.

Outputs
- Strategic plans, especially the service strategy
- Tactical plans
- Strategy review schedules and documentation
- Mission and vision statements
- Policies
- Strategic requirements for new services, and input into which existing services need to be changed.

Interfaces
- **Service portfolio management** Provides the guidelines and framework within which the service portfolio will be defined and managed.
- **Financial management for IT services** Provides the financial information and tools to enable prioritization of actions and plans, and indicates what types of returns are required and where investments need to be made.
- **Service design** Enables measurement and evaluation of the services being designed, and identifies any policies and constraints that must be taken into account when designing services, and a clear prioritization of work.
- **Service transition** Enables service transition to prioritize and evaluate the services that are built to ensure they meet the original intent and strategic requirements of the services. Any variations detected during service transition are fed back so that the existing strategy can be reviewed.
- **Knowledge management** Structures the information used to make strategic decisions.
- **Service operation** Operational tools and processes must be aligned to the strategic objectives and desired business outcomes, and monitoring of operational environments should be instrumented so that the execution of operational activities indicates the effectiveness of the strategy.

- **CSI** Helps to evaluate whether the strategy has been executed effectively, and whether it has met its objectives. Any deviations are reported to enable process improvements or strategy adjustments.

2.3.4.7 Critical success factors and key performance indicators (SS 4.1.8)

Table 2.4 includes some sample CSFs for strategy management for IT services, followed by a small number of typical KPIs that support each CSF. Achievement against KPIs should be monitored and used to identify opportunities for improvement, which should be logged in the CSI register for evaluation and possible implementation.

Table 2.4 Examples of critical success factors and key performance indicators for strategy management for IT services

Critical success factor	Key performance indicator
The ability to identify constraints on the ability of the service provider to meet business outcomes, and to deliver and manage services – and the ability to eliminate these constraints or reduce their impact	Number of corrective actions taken to remove constraints, and the result of those actions on the achievement of strategic objectives
The service provider has a clear understanding of their perspective, and it is reviewed regularly to ensure ongoing relevance	Vision and mission statements have been defined and all staff members have been trained
	Each business unit has a strategic plan

Table continues

Table 2.4 *continued*

Critical success factor	Key performance indicator
The service provider has a clear understanding of how it positions itself to ensure competitive advantage	Every strategic and tactical plan contains a statement of how the contents of the plan support the competitive advantage of the service provider
	External service providers win a defined percentage of all proposed business deals within the identified market space
	For internal service providers, funding is made available to support the strategic initiatives, and an ROI can be demonstrated
The ability to translate strategic plans into tactical and operational plans that are executed by each organizational unit	Each tactical and operational plan is identified by the strategic plans they support, and changes to the strategy are managed through change control to ensure that tactical and operational plans are aligned

Critical success factor	Key performance indicator
Changes to the internal and external environments are identified and adjustments made to strategies and related documents	Number of strategic objectives that are not met – identified by CSI activities
	Deviation from activities and patterns identified in the strategy
	Number of changes to internal and external environments identified, compared with the number of changes made to strategy documents

2.3.4.8   Challenges and risks (SS 4.1.9) ✗

Challenges

■ Strategy management for IT services is conducted at the wrong level in the organization – it should be driven by senior executives, and each organizational unit should follow through with the production of a strategic, tactical and operational plan that is a subset of the enterprise strategy

■ Lack of accurate information about the external environment

■ Lack of support by stakeholders

■ Lack of the appropriate tools or a lack of understanding of how to use the tools and techniques identified in this section

■ Operational targets need to be matched to the strategic objectives. Failure to do so will result in operational managers striving to achieve targets that are not in support of the strategy.

Risks

- A flawed governance model that allows managers to decide on whether to implement all aspects of a strategy, or to deviate from the strategy for shorter-term goals
- Short-term priorities override the directives of the strategy
- Making strategic decisions when there is missing information about the internal or external environments, or using information that is incorrect or misleading (i.e. information that has not been validated)
- Choosing the wrong strategy – feedback to the service management process at all stages is key so that incorrect decisions can be detected early and corrected
- Strategies are seen as an exercise that happens once a year and that has no bearing on what happens for the rest of the year.

2.3.5 Demand management (SS 4.4) ✗

2.3.5.1 Purpose and objectives (SS 4.4.1) ✗

The purpose of the demand management process is to understand, anticipate and influence customer demand for services, and the process by which sufficient capacity to meet the demand is provisioned.

The objectives of demand management include:

- Understand the levels of demand that will be placed on a service, by identification and analysis of PBA (see section 2.2.4)
- Understand the profiles of demand through analysis of the user profiles of the different types of users of each service
- Ensure services are defined to meet the expected PBA

■ Ensure that adequate resources are available to meet the demands of the service – this is achieved through close collaboration with capacity management.

2.3.5.2 Scope (SS 4.4.2)

The scope of demand management is to identify and analyse the PBA that initiate demand for services, and to identify and analyse how different types of user influence the demand for services.

Demand management activities should include:

■ Identifying and analysing PBA associated with services
■ Identifying user profiles and analysing their service usage patterns
■ Identifying, agreeing and implementing measures to influence demand together with capacity management. This is sometimes called the 'management of demand'.

Demand management is active in every stage of the service lifecycle, and works closely with several other processes, especially capacity management.

The scopes of capacity and demand management seem to overlap, with demand management as an aspect of capacity management. This is an over-simplification of both processes. Both are concerned with achieving the same business outcomes and optimizing investment. However, demand management focuses primarily on the business and user aspects of providing services, whereas capacity management focuses primarily on the resourcing and technology aspects.

2.3.5.3   Value to business (SS 4.4.3) ✗

The main value of demand management is to achieve a balance between the cost of a service and the value of the business outcomes it supports. The other service strategy processes define the linkage between (and the investment required for) business outcomes, services, resources and capabilities. Demand management improves the understanding of how, when and to what level these elements interact, enabling executives to evaluate the real investment required to achieve business outcomes at varying levels of activity.

2.3.5.4   Principles and basic concepts (SS 4.4.4) ✗

Supply and demand

Consumption produces demand and production consumes demand in a highly synchronized pattern. Demand management is the process by which a service provider gathers a clear understanding of the PBA of each of its customers that generate demand, and seeks to influence how and when these demand patterns are formed.

This cycle of demand and supply will only function effectively while the service assets have available capacity. For this reason, a major part of demand management is to understand the potential demand, and the impact of the demand on the service assets to allow capacity management to manage service assets (and investments) towards optimal performance and cost.

Gearing service assets

The balance of supply and demand is achieved by gearing the service assets to meet the dynamic patterns of demand on services, both responding to demand as it occurs and anticipating the demand by identifying the signals of increasing or decreasing demand and defining a mechanism to scale investment and supply as required.

Managing service assets according to demand involves a number of service management actions, including the following:

■ Identifying the services (through service portfolio management)
■ Quantifying the PBA
■ Specifying the appropriate architecture to deal with the type and quantity of demand
■ Capacity and availability planning to ensure that the right service assets are available at the right time and are performing at the right levels
■ Performance management and tuning service assets to deal with variations in demand.

Demand management through the lifecycle

To be fully effective, demand management needs to be active throughout the service lifecycle. It might be tempting to assume that processes that are active in each stage of the lifecycle will address demand issues. However, if demand management is not consciously coordinated and managed, this will only happen on an ad hoc, reactive basis.

2.3.5.5   Process activities, methods and techniques (SS 4.4.5)

The following activities, methods and techniques can be selected and applied as needed to perform demand management:

■ **Identify sources of demand forecasting** Identify any documents, reports or information that can provide insight to support forecasting.

- **PBA** Represent the dynamics of the business and include interactions with customers, suppliers, partners and other stakeholders (see section 2.2.4).
- **User profiles (UPs)** Based on roles and responsibilities within organizations. Each UP can be associated with one or more PBA, allowing aggregations and relations between diverse PBA. UPs are constructed using one or more predefined PBA under change control. When PBA and UPs are used to define demand, service providers can serve demand with appropriately matched services, service levels and service assets.
- **Activity-based demand management** Analysing and tracking the activity patterns of the business process enables prediction of demand for the IT services that support the process. This enables prediction of demand for the underlying service assets that support those services. Activity-based demand management can consolidate demand patterns to ensure that the business plans of customers are synchronized with service management plans, such as the capacity plan.
- **Develop differentiated offerings** Analysis of PBA may identify that different levels of performance are required at different times, or different combinations of utility. In these cases, it is important to work with service portfolio management to define service packages that meet the variations in PBA.
- **Management of operational demand** To manage or influence the demand where services or resources are being over-utilized.

2.3.5.6   Triggers, inputs, outputs and interfaces (SS 4.4.6)

Triggers

- A request for a new service, or change to an existing service
- Creation of a new service
- A service model needs to be defined, and PBA and/or UPs must be defined

- Utilization rates are causing potential performance issues, or a potential breach of an SLA
- An exception has occurred to forecast PBA.

Inputs

- Initiative to create a new service, or to change an existing service via service portfolio management or change management
- Service models
- The customer portfolio, service portfolio and customer agreement portfolio
- Charging models
- Chargeable items
- Service improvement opportunities and plans.

Outputs

- UPs
- PBA
- Policies for management of demand when resources are over-utilized
- Policies for how to deal with situations where service utilization is higher or lower than anticipated by the customer
- Documentation of options for differentiated offerings that can be used to create service packages.

Interfaces

- **Strategy management for IT services** Identifies the key business outcomes and business activities that are used to establish PBA and user profiles.
- **Service portfolio management** Uses information from demand management to create and evaluate service models, to establish and forecast utilization requirements and to identify the different types of user of the service.

- **Financial management for IT services** Helps to forecast the cost of providing the demand based on forecast PBA, identify measures to regulate demand when there is over-utilization of the service and identify the relative costs of each differentiated offering.
- **Business relationship management** Is the primary source of information about the business activities of the customer and is useful in validating the user profiles and differentiated service offerings before they are confirmed in the customer and service portfolios.
- **SLM** Helps to formalize agreements in which the customer commits to levels of utilization, and the service provider commits to levels of performance. Demand management works with SLM to define policies for how to deal with variances in supply and demand.
- **Capacity management** Works with demand management to define exactly how to match supply and demand in the design and operation of the service. Capacity management monitors the actual utilization of services and works with demand management to understand trends of utilization and how to adjust the services for future use.
- **Availability management** Uses information about PBA to determine when service availability is most important, useful for performing service outage analysis and project service availability reporting.

2.3.5.7   Critical success factors and key performance indicators (SS 4.4.8)

Table 2.5 includes some sample CSFs for demand management, followed by a small number of typical KPIs that support each CSF. Achievement against KPIs should be monitored and used to identify opportunities for improvement, which should be logged in the CSI register for evaluation and possible implementation.

Table 2.5 Examples of critical success factors and key performance indicators for demand management

Critical success factor	Key performance indicator
The service provider has identified and analysed the PBA and is able to use these to understand the levels of demand that will be placed on a service	PBA are defined for each relevant service
	PBA have been translated into workload information by capacity management
The service provider has defined and analysed user profiles and is able to use these to understand the typical profiles of demand for services from different types of user	Documented user profiles exist and each contains a demand profile for the services used by that type of user
A process exists whereby services are designed to meet the PBA and meet business outcomes	Demand management activities are routinely included as part of defining the service portfolio
An interface with capacity management to ensure that adequate resources are available at the appropriate levels of capacity to meet the demand for services	Capacity plans include details of PBA and corresponding workloads
	Utilization monitors show balanced workloads

Table continues

Table 2.5 *continued*

Critical success factor	Key performance indicator
There is a means to manage situations where demand for a service exceeds the capacity to deliver it	Techniques to manage demand have been documented in capacity plans and, where appropriate, in SLAs
	Differential charging has resulted in a more even demand on the service over time

2.3.5.8   Challenges and risks (SS 4.4.9) ✗

Challenges

- The availability of information about business activities – especially if demand management is not included in the overall set of requirements and has to be collected separately. Customers have a limited tolerance for how many people gather information about their service requirements
- Customers might find it difficult to break down individual activities that make sense to the service provider. Business relationship management should be able to assist in making this translation
- Lack of a formal service portfolio management process or service portfolio. This will make it difficult to understand the business requirements, relative value and priority of services, and will mean that demand management information might be recorded on an *ad hoc* basis, often with little coordination and duplicate effort.

Risks

- Lack of, or inaccurate, configuration management information, which makes it difficult to estimate the impact of changing demand on the service provider's infrastructure and applications
- SLM is not able to obtain commitments to minimum or maximum utilization levels, and it is therefore difficult to commit to levels of service. This situation often results in higher than necessary levels of investment to enable the service provider to keep ahead of demand – even when not essential.

2.4   TECHNOLOGY CONSIDERATIONS (SS 7.1) ✔

2.4.1   Service automation ✔

Service automation can improve the utility and warranty of services, providing advantages such as:

- It is easier to adjust the capacity of automated resources in response to changes in demand volumes and patterns
- Automated resources make it easier to respond to changes in requirements, and enable greater flexibility to serve demand across time zones and out of normal business hours
- Automated systems produce high degrees of consistency
- Scheduling, routing and allocation of resources is complex and time consuming and an ideal candidate for automation
- Automation enables effective capture, codification and distribution of knowledge throughout the service provider's organization in a consistent and secure manner, and reduces the risk of knowledge being lost through staff movement.

Automation of service processes can significantly contribute to improved service quality and reduced service costs and risks. Service management can particularly benefit from automation in the areas of:

- Design and modelling
- Service catalogue
- Pattern recognition and analysis
- Classification, prioritization and routing
- Detection and monitoring
- Optimization.

2.4.2   Service analytics and instrumentation ✔

Service analytics techniques are used throughout service management to apply context and understanding to service data captured from multiple sources.

Raw service data by itself is not particularly useful. Analysis of this data in terms of questioning who the service data relates to, what it relates to, when it was captured and from where, enables the service provider to form useful information on its services and customers. Further examination of the information enables the service provider to identify and understand patterns in the information, such as:

- How does this incident affect the service?
- How is the business impacted?
- How do we respond?

Figure 2.7 shows the Data-to-Information-to-Knowledge-to-Wisdom structure (DIKW), which results from service analytics (SS 7.1.2).

Figure 2.7 The flow from data to wisdom

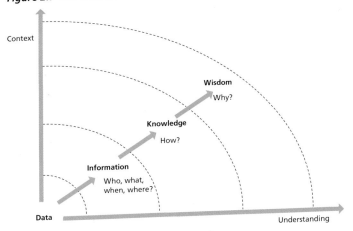

Most organizations have some form of monitoring instrumentation to capture data about the state of elements within the service infrastructure. Instrumentation techniques include:

■ **Asynchronous capture** Passive listeners scanning for alerts
■ **External source** Compilation of data from external sources such as service desk tickets, supplier notifications and enterprise resource planning systems
■ **Manual generation** Manually create or alter an event
■ **Polling** Monitoring systems actively interrogate functional elements on a regular basis
■ **Synthetic transactions** Simulation of end-user experience through known transactions.

Collection of instrumentation data is vital first step, but the behaviours of the component elements of a service need to be aggregated so that the overall behaviour of a service can be understood. Therefore, the instrumentation data needs to be put into context to understand its relevance and significance. Information is built from understanding the data itself and the relationships between the pieces of data.

Service analytics and instrumentation are critical to event management, where usable and actionable information is produced from monitoring data. Common event management techniques include:

- **Compression** Consolidation of multiple identical alerts into a single alert
- **Correlation** Analysis to identify if multiple alerts from various sources happening during a short period of time have any relationship
- **Filtering** Applying rules to a single alert source over some period of time
- **Intelligent monitoring** Applying adaptive instrumentation that automatically tunes the monitoring techniques according to system status
- **Roll-up** Compression of alerts through the use of hierarchical collection structures
- **Verification** Active confirmation of an actual incident.

3   Service design

For services to provide true value to the business, they must be designed with the business objectives in mind. Service design is the stage in the lifecycle that turns a service strategy into a plan for delivering the business objectives.

ITIL Service Design provides

■ Guidance for the design and development of services and service management practices
■ Design principles and methods for converting strategic objectives into portfolios of services and service assets.

3.1   PURPOSE, OBJECTIVES, SCOPE AND VALUE OF SERVICE DESIGN

3.1.1   Purpose and objectives (SD 1.1.1) ✔

The purpose of service design is to:

■ Design IT services, governing IT practices, processes and policies
■ Realize the service provider's strategy
■ Facilitate the introduction of services
■ Ensure quality service delivery, customer satisfaction and cost-effective service provision.

The objective is to:

■ Design IT services so effectively that minimum improvement during their lifecycle will be required
■ Embed continual improvement in all service design activities to ensure that solutions become even more effective over time
■ Identify changing trends in the business that may offer improvement opportunities.

3.1.2 Scope (SD 1.1.2) ✔

Service design starts with a set of new or changed business requirements and ends with the development of a service solution designed to meet those requirements.

There are five aspects to service design, covering the design of:

- Service solutions for new or changed services
- Management information systems and tools
- Technology architectures and management architectures
- The processes required
- Measurement methods and metrics.

3.1.3 Value to business (SD 1.1.4) ✔

Good service design makes it possible to deliver quality, cost-effective services and to ensure that the business requirements are being met.

A standard and consistent service design approach:

- Reduces total cost of ownership (TCO)
- Improves the quality, consistency and performance of service
- Eases the implementation of new or changed services
- Improves alignment with business needs and with customer values and strategies
- Improves IT governance
- Improves effectiveness of service management and IT processes
- Improves information and decision-making.

3.2   KEY PRINCIPLES

3.2.1   The four Ps of service design (SD 3.1.5) ✔

It is key to recognize the importance of the four Ps to successful service provision:

- People
- Processes
- Products (services, technology and tools)
- Partners (supplier, manufacturers and vendors).

Many designs, plans and projects fail through a lack of preparation and management. The implementation of ITSM as a practice is about preparing and planning the effective and efficient use of the four Ps.

3.2.2   Balanced service design (SD 3.3) ✘

At its heart service design involves a delicate balancing act. Initially this is between the functionality requirements and the performance requirements, service utility and service warranty. Service design must understand and evaluate the implications for the resulting business value of the service in finding the balance.

Next the realities of resource availability must be considered. What technology, people and skills will be required? How much budget is available to move through the service lifecycle from transition into operation? What are the forecast business-as-usual costs for running the service?

Finally the constraints of the timescale available to move the service into operation must be taken into account.

Good service design must balance all of the above to ensure an effective end result.

3.2.3   The five design aspects (SD 3.1.1) ✔

Service design takes into consideration five major aspects of service provision, as listed in section 3.1.2, for which the design activities must be carried out.

3.2.3.1   Designing service solutions (SD 3.7.1) ✔

A formal and structured approach is required to produce a service with the right balance of functionality and cost within agreed timescales. This approach must be iterative/incremental to ensure the service delivered meets the evolving and changing needs of the business.

The areas to be considered include:

- Analyse the business requirements
- Explore opportunities for re-use
- Produce service solution designs
- Create and maintain the service acceptance criteria (SAC)
- Evaluate and cost alternative designs
- Agree the expenditure, budgets and timelines through to deployment of the service
- Re-evaluate and confirm the business benefits
- Agree the preferred solution and its planned outcomes and targets
- Ensure the solution is in line with strategies, policies, architecture and make proposals for change if not
- Ensure corporate and IT governance and security controls are taken into account
- Complete an organizational readiness assessment
- Identify requirements for suppliers and supporting contracts
- Assemble the service design package (SDP).

3.2.3.2 Designing management information systems and tools (SD 3.7.2) ✔

The most effective way of managing all aspects of services through their lifecycle is by using appropriate management systems and tools, including:

- Service portfolio
- Service knowledge management system (SKMS)
- Configuration management system (CMS)
- Capacity management information system (CMIS)
- Availability management information system (AMIS)
- Security management information system (SMIS)
- Service continuity management information system.

It is important that the design and development of these systems and tools is undertaken in the same way as for any other IT service to ensure that they meet the needs of all stakeholders.

The service portfolio is the most critical management system used to support all processes, and describes a provider's services in terms of business value. It contains details of all services within the service pipeline, the service catalogue or the retired services catalogue, dependent on the current stage of a service in the service lifecycle.

3.2.3.3 Designing technology architectures and management architectures (SD 3.7.3) ✔

Architectural design within an IT organization provides the strategic blueprints for the development and deployment of an IT infrastructure that will satisfy the needs of the business. It involves the development and maintenance of:

- IT policies
- Strategies
- Architectures

■ Designs
■ Plans
■ Processes.

An architecture for any system should consider its constituent
components; their relationship to each other and how they
interact; the relationship between the system and its environment;
the design principles that inform, guide and constrain its
structure and operation, as well as its future development.

Figure 3.1 Architectural relationships

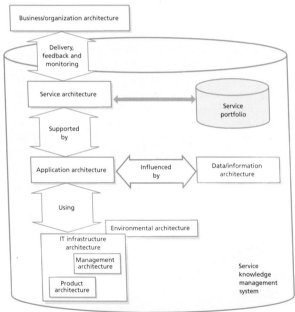

Service design should consider the service architecture and its four supporting architectures – the data, applications, infrastructure and environment as illustrated in Figure 3.1 – plus the management architecture.

The five areas to consider when designing a suitable management architecture are:

- Business requirements
- People, roles and activities
- Processes and procedures
- Management tools
- Technology.

The management architecture needs to be designed top-down to ensure that the overall result is designed with the needs of the business as the key driver for the other areas.

Management architectures need to be business-aligned, not technology-driven.

Designing processes (SD 3.7.4) ✔

Process theory and practice is the basis for the design of ITIL processes that are used in the service lifecycle.

A process model enables understanding and helps to articulate the distinctive features of a process.

Each process is owned by a process owner, who is accountable for the process, its improvement and for ensuring it meets its objectives.

Process outputs are expected to conform to operational norms, and where this is the case, the process can be considered to be effective. If the activities are carried out with a minimum use of resources the process can be considered efficient.

Designing measurement methods and metrics (SD 3.7.5) ✔

To effectively manage processes and their outcomes they have to be measured. The measurements and metrics selected need to reflect the goals and objectives of the process being measured.

Process measurements need to be appropriate to the level of capability and maturity of the processes being measured. Immature processes are incapable of supporting sophisticated measurements.

Take care when selecting measurements as they will drive behavioural changes in the organization. Selection of the wrong metric can lead to undesired changes in behaviour, in contradiction to the goals and objectives of the process.

Where possible, metrics need to be driven by organizational goals and developed to operate in a hierarchical way – a metrics tree – so that detailed technical operational and process metrics, at the lowest levels, can be aggregated and reported at a higher level to demonstrate service performance against SLAs. These can then be aggregated to the next level to produce a management dashboard, giving an overall picture of performance. This information can then be used at a higher level again to demonstrate performance against organizational goals and objectives. The balanced scorecard is an example of a tool that can be used to develop a set of organizational metrics and measures in this way.

3.2.4 The service design package (SD Appendix A) ✔

> **Definition: service design package** ✔
>
> Document(s) defining all aspects of an IT service and its requirements through each stage of its lifecycle. A service design package is produced for each new IT service, major change, or IT service retirement.

The service design package (SDP) is the significant product of the service design stage. It is assembled using the output from the various processes, methods and techniques employed throughout service design, and is the foundation document supporting the subsequent transition, operation and continual improvement of the new or changed service.

At a high level the SDP includes the following:

- Requirements
- Service design
- Organizational readiness assessment
- Service lifecycle plans including programme, transition and operational acceptance plans
- Service acceptance criteria (SAC).

3.2.5 Delivery model options (SD 3.11.1) ✘

As part of the service design, and a major input to the SDP, an organizational readiness assessment is carried out. This assesses the current capability of the organization against the requirements of the new or changed service.

A number of service-sourcing strategies are available to fill any gaps identified:

- ◼ **Insourcing** Using internal resources
- ◼ **Outsourcing** Using the resources of an external organization
- ◼ **Co-sourcing or multi-sourcing** A number of organizations working together to provide key parts of the solution
- ◼ **Partnership** Formal arrangements between two or more organizations to work together in a strategic partnership to deliver a service, sharing the rewards
- ◼ **Business process outsourcing (BPO)** One organization takes over the provision of an entire business function on behalf of another
- ◼ **Application service provision** An application service provider (ASP) allows access to shared computer-based services to another – sometimes called 'on-demand services'
- ◼ **Knowledge process outsourcing (KPO)** One organization provides domain-based, specialized services for another
- ◼ **'Cloud'** Specific predefined services, usually on demand. Services are usually standard, but can be customized to a specific organization if there is enough demand for the service
- ◼ **Multi-vendor sourcing** This type of sourcing involves sourcing different services from different vendors, often using multiple options from the above.

Each of these sourcing options comes with its own pros and cons that need to be considered, along with the potential for added complexity and increased risk, when deciding on an appropriate delivery model as part of the service design.

3.3   PROCESSES AND ACTIVITIES

3.3.1   Design coordination (SD 4.1) ✔

3.3.1.1   Purpose and objectives (SD 4.1.1) ✔

The purpose of design coordination is to ensure the goals and objectives of the design stage are met. It provides a single point of coordination and control for all activities and processes within this stage of the service lifecycle.

The objectives of the design coordination process are to:

■ Ensure the consistent design of appropriate services, service management information systems, architectures, technology, processes, information and metrics to meet current and evolving business needs and requirements
■ Plan and coordinate all design activities
■ Produce SDPs based on service charters and change requests
■ Ensure that appropriate service designs are produced and that they are handed over to service transition as agreed
■ Manage the interfaces with service strategy and service transition
■ Improve the efficiency and effectiveness of service design activities and processes.

3.3.1.2   Scope (SD 4.1.2) ✔

The scope of design coordination includes all design activity.

Some design efforts will be part of a project and others will be managed through the change process alone, without a formally defined project. Typically, major changes require the most attention from design coordination but any change that could benefit from design coordination may be included.

Each organization should define criteria to determine the level of attention to be applied in design coordination for each design.

3.3.1.3   Value to business (SD 4.1.3) ✗

The design coordination process ensures the production of consistent quality solution designs and SDPs that will provide the desired business outcomes.

3.3.1.4   Principles and basic concepts (SD 4.1.4) ✗

The service provider should define policies to determine the level of coordination to be provided for different service design efforts. The policy should establish the required level of documentation.

Balance and prioritization

Care must be taken to balance the goal of a comprehensive design that addresses all aspects of utility and warranty with the risk of setting up excessively bureaucratic standards and requirements at the expense of consistently returning better services.

Integration with project management

Many major design efforts are managed as part of a project and rely heavily on the service design experience of the project manager. Design coordination should ensure that the procedures and products needed for design success are integrated into the overall project management methodology.

3.3.1.5 Process activities, methods and techniques (SD 4.1.5) ✗

Design coordination activities fall into two categories (see Figure 3.2):

- Activities relating to the overall service design lifecycle stage. These activities may be performed by design coordination process manager(s).
- Activities relating to each individual design. These activities may be performed by a project manager or other individual with direct responsibility for the project or change. The design coordination process manager provides assistance and guidance.

Figure 3.2 Design coordination activities

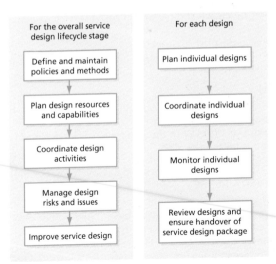

3.3.1.6   Triggers, inputs, outputs and interfaces (SD 4.1.6) ✗

Triggers

- Changes in the business requirements and services
- Requests for change (RFCs)
- New programmes or projects
- Revision of the overall IT strategy.

Inputs

- Service charters for new or changed services
- Change requests from any stage of the service lifecycle
- Business information from the organization's business and IT strategy and from business impact analysis (BIA).

Outputs

- A comprehensive and consistent set of service designs and SDPs
- Revised enterprise architecture
- Revised management systems, processes, measurement and metrics methods.

Interfaces

- **Service strategy** Using information contained within the IT strategy and service portfolio.
- **Service transition** With the handover of the design of service solutions within the SDP.

3.3.1.7   Critical success factors and key performance indicators (SD 4.1.8) ✗

Table 3.1 includes some sample critical success factors (CSFs) for design coordination, followed by a small number of typical key performance indicators (KPIs) that support each CSF. Achievement against KPIs should be monitored and used to identify opportunities for improvement, which should be logged in the CSI register for evaluation and possible implementation.

Table 3.1 Examples of critical success factors and key performance indicators for design coordination

Critical success factor	Key performance indicator
Accurate and consistent SDPs	Reduction in the number of subsequent revisions of the content of SDPs
Managing conflicting demands for shared resources	Reduced number of issues caused by conflict for service design resources
New and changed services meet customer expectations	Percentage increase in the number of transitioned services that consistently achieve the agreed service level targets

3.3.1.8   Challenges and risks (SD 4.1.9)

Challenges

- Maintaining high-quality SDPs across the complex landscape of different businesses, services and infrastructure
- Ensuring that sufficient resources are devoted to design coordination activities
- Developing common design practices that produce the required quality designs without introducing unnecessary bureaucracy.

Risks

- Lack of skills and knowledge
- Lack of involvement from the business
- Poorly defined or unclear business priorities and requirements.

3.3.2 Service level management (SD 4.3) ☑

3.3.2.1 Purpose and objectives (SD 4.3.1) ✓

The purpose of the service level management (SLM) process is to ensure that all current and planned IT services are delivered to agreed achievable targets.

The objectives of SLM are to:

- Define, document, agree, monitor, measure, report and review the level of IT services provided
- Improve the relationship and communication with the business and customers
- Ensure that specific and measurable targets are developed
- Monitor and improve customer satisfaction
- Ensure a clear and unambiguous expectation of the level of service to be delivered
- Ensure continual improvement to the levels of service, even when all agreed targets are met.

3.3.2.2 Scope (SD 4.3.2) ✓

SLM acts to represent the service provider to the business and the business to the service provider.

It manages the expectations and perceptions of the business, customers and users, and ensures that the service provided is in line with those expectations. Its focus extends beyond currently delivered services to involvement in the design of new or changed services, producing and agreeing the service level requirements for these services.

3.3.2.3   Value to business (SD 4.3.3)

SLM provides a reliable communication channel and a trusted relationship between the customers and business representatives. It supplies the business with agreed service targets and the required management information to ensure those targets have been met.

3.3.2.4   Principles and basic concepts (SD 4.3.4)

Service level requirements

Service level requirements (SLRs) define the customer requirements for an IT service based on business objectives, and are used to negotiate service level agreements (SLAs).

Service level agreements (SLAs)

> **Definition: service level agreement**
>
> An agreement between an IT service provider and a customer. A service level agreement describes the IT service, documents service level targets, and specifies the responsibilities of the IT service provider and the customer. A single agreement may cover multiple IT services or multiple customers.

SLAs provide the basis for managing the relationship between the service provider and the customer.

SLM develops SLAs for all services and ensures the service continues to be delivered in line with the agreements made in the SLA.

Service level agreement monitoring (SLAM) chart

A service level agreement monitoring (SLAM) chart monitors and reports achievements against service level targets. Such a chart is typically colour-coded to show whether each agreed service level target has been met, missed or nearly missed during each of the previous 12 months. Figure 6.3 shows an example of an SLAM chart.

Service level agreement frameworks ✔

When designing SLA frameworks, options available include:

- **Service-based SLAs** The SLA describes a specific IT service to be delivered.
- **Customer-based SLAs** All IT services delivered to a specific customer are described.
- **Multi-level SLAs** For example, from corporate down through customer to service, where the agreements at each level are inherited by those at the next. This helps with ongoing maintenance, making the SLAs easier to work with. The information at the higher levels is subject to less frequent change and is not repeated in every lower-level SLA.

Where service delivery relies on supporting services provided either by other departments or by external suppliers, SLM ensures that operational level agreements (OLAs) and contracts are in place to underpin the service delivery targets in the SLA.

Definition: operational level agreement ✔

An agreement between an IT service provider and another part of the same organization. It supports the IT service provider's delivery of IT services to customers and defines the goods or services to be provided and the responsibilities of both parties.

Definition: underpinning contract ✔

A contract between an IT service provider and a third party. The third party provides goods or services that support delivery of an IT service to a customer. The underpinning contract defines targets and responsibilities that are required to meet agreed service level targets in one or more service level agreements.

Service review ✔

This constitutes meetings held on a regular basis with customers (or their representatives) to review the service achievement in the previous period and to preview any issues for the coming period. The customer and provider should be actioned as appropriate to improve weak areas where targets are not being met. Analysis of the cost and impact of service breaches provides valuable input and justification of service improvement plan (SIP) activities and actions.

Service improvement plan (SIP) ✔

Definition: service improvement plan ✔

A formal plan to implement improvements to a process or IT service.

Service level management and business relationship management ✔

While SLM focuses on ensuring agreed levels of service are provided to the customer and users, business relationship management focuses on a more strategic level – to ensure the service provider is meeting the customer's overall needs.

3.3.2.5 Process activities, methods and techniques (SD 4.3.5) ✔

The key activities for SLM are:

- Design SLA frameworks
- Determine, document and agree requirements for new services and produce SLRs
- Negotiate, document, agree, monitor and report on SLAs for operational services
- Conduct service reviews and instigate improvements within an overall SIP
- Collate, measure and improve customer satisfaction
- Review and revise SLAs, OLAs, service scope and underpinning agreements.

3.3.2.6 Triggers, inputs, outputs and interfaces (SD 4.3.6) ✔

Triggers

- Changes in the service portfolio
- New or changed SLRs, SLAs, OLAs or contracts
- Service breaches or threatened breaches
- Periodic activities – reviewing, reporting and customer satisfaction surveys
- Changes in strategy or policy.

Inputs

- Business requirements
- Strategies, policies and constraints from service strategy
- The service portfolio and the service catalogue
- Customer and user feedback
- Improvement opportunities from the CSI register.

Outputs
- Service reports
- Service improvement opportunities
- SIP
- SLRs, SLAs, and OLAs.

Interfaces
- **Business relationship management** Provides a full understanding of the needs and priorities of the business. Ensures customers are appropriately involved and represented.
- **Service catalogue management** Provides information about services and their interfaces and dependencies. Identifies customers/business units that need to be engaged by SLM.
- **Incident management** Provides data to demonstrate performance against SLA targets. Ensures incidents are resolved in line with SLA targets.
- **Supplier management** Ensures supplier and contractual targets align with SLAs.
- **Availability, capacity, IT service continuity and information security management (ISM)** Support definition of service level targets related to the specific area of responsibility.
- **Design coordination** Ensures that the overall service design activities are completed successfully.

3.3.2.7   Critical success factors and key performance indicators (SD 4.3.8)

Table 3.2 includes some sample CSFs for SLM, followed by a small number of typical KPIs that support each CSF. Achievement against KPIs should be monitored and used to identify opportunities for improvement, which should be logged in the CSI register for evaluation and possible implementation.

Table 3.2 Examples of critical success factors and key performance indicators for service level management

Critical success factor	Key performance indicator
Managing the overall quality of IT services required both in the number and level of services provided and managed	Percentage reduction in SLA targets threatened
	Percentage increase in customer satisfaction
Deliver the service as previously agreed at affordable costs	Total number and percentage of fully documented SLAs in place
	Percentage reduction in the costs associated with service provision
Manage the interface with the business and the users	Increased percentage of services covered by SLAs
	Documented and agreed SLM processes and procedures are in place

3.3.2.8   Challenges and risks (SD 4.3.9) ✗

Challenges

■ Identifying and involving the right people within the customer base when drafting and agreeing the SLA. The manager paying for the service may have very different targets and requirements from the staff that use the service on a day-to-day basis. It is important that all appropriate and relevant views are gathered and considered when agreeing the SLA

- If the organization is new to SLM, carefully select an appropriate service to start with. Avoid selecting one that is too complex or 'emotional'
- The SLA needs to be an agreement on both sides. Ensure appropriate involvement from service delivery staff, especially the key functions within service operation.

Risks

- A lack of accurate input or of involvement and commitment from the business
- A lack of appropriate tools and resources to carry out the process
- Business and customer measurements are too difficult to measure and improve, so are not recorded.

3.3.3 Service catalogue management (SD 4.2) ✔

> **Definition: service catalogue**
>
> A database or structured document with information about all live IT services, including those available for deployment. The service catalogue is part of the service portfolio and contains information about two types of IT service: customer-facing services that are visible to the business; and supporting services required by the service provider to deliver customer-facing services.

3.3.3.1 Purpose and objectives (SD 4.2.1) ✔

The service catalogue is a single source of consistent information on all of the agreed services. The objective of service catalogue management is to manage the information contained within the service catalogue and to ensure that it is accurate and current.

3.3.3.2   Scope (SD 4.2.2) ✔

The scope is to provide and maintain accurate information on all services that are being transitioned, or have been transitioned, to the live environment.

3.3.3.3   Value to business (SD 4.2.3) ✗

The service catalogue provides the business with an accurate, consistent picture of the IT services in use, how they are intended to be used, the business processes they enable and the associated service levels.

3.3.3.4   Principles and basic concepts (SD 4.2.4) ✔

The service catalogue is part of the service portfolio. The service catalogue contains details of all services from the point they are 'chartered' as part of the service strategy stage. It contains details of services as they progress through the design, transition and operation stages of the service lifecycle.

The service catalogue is also used by many other service management processes to support their activities and to provide the basis for analysis across the full scope of delivered services.

It is recommended that a service provider defines two different views of the service catalogue. This is referred to as a two-view service catalogue:

■ **Business/customer service catalogue** ✔ Contains details of the IT services delivered to the customers (customer-facing services), links to the business units and the business processes they support and provides the customer view of the service catalogue.

■ **Technical/supporting service catalogue** ✔ Contains details of the supporting IT services delivered, links to the customer-facing services and configuration items (CIs) and other supporting services necessary to deliver the service.

The number of views defined depends on the audiences to be addressed and the uses to which the catalogue will be put. For instance, a three-view service catalogue may be created to distinguish the customer-facing services available to different customers, or different types of customer, e.g. wholesale versus retail customers.

3.3.3.5 Process activities, methods and techniques (SD 4.2.5) ✗

Key activities for service catalogue management are:

■ Agree and document service definitions
■ Interface with service portfolio management (service portfolio management) to agree the contents of the service portfolio and the service catalogue
■ Produce and maintain the service catalogue
■ Interface with the business and IT service continuity management (ITSCM) to understand the links between business processes and the IT services
■ Interface with support teams and service asset and configuration management (SACM) to understand the relationships with supporting services, components and CIs
■ Interface with business relationship management and SLM to ensure information is aligned to the business.

3.3.3.6 Triggers, inputs, outputs and interfaces (SD 4.2.6) ✗

Triggers

■ Changes in the business requirements
■ Changes in the services.

Inputs
- Business information from the business and IT strategy
- BIA
- Business requirements
- RFCs.

Outputs
- Updates to the service portfolio
- Updates to RFCs
- The service catalogue.

Interfaces
- **Service portfolio management** Determines which services will be chartered and so included in the service catalogue.
- **Business relationship management** Ensures the relationship between the customer and the service is clearly defined.
- **SACM** Ensures information in the service catalogue and in the CMS are appropriately linked together.

3.3.3.7 Critical success factors and key performance indicators (SD 4.2.8) ✗

Table 3.3 includes some sample CSFs for service catalogue management, followed by a small number of typical KPIs that support each CSF. Achievement against KPIs should be monitored and used to identify opportunities for improvement, which should be logged in the CSI register for evaluation and possible implementation.

Table 3.3 Examples of critical success factors and key performance indicators for service catalogue management

Critical success factor	Key performance indicator
An accurate service catalogue	Increase in the number of services recorded in the service catalogue as a percentage of those being delivered
Business users' awareness of the services being provided	Percentage increase in completeness of the customer-facing view(s) of services against operational services
IT staff awareness of the technology supporting services	Percentage increase in completeness of the supporting services against the IT components that make up those services

3.3.3.8   Challenges and risks (SD 4.2.9)

Challenges

- The main challenge is in maintaining the service catalogue, with the business and technical views, to ensure that it is current and consistent.

Risks

- Inaccuracy of the data in the catalogue
- Poor acceptance of the service catalogue and its usage in all operational processes
- Insufficient tools and resources required to maintain the catalogue

- Poor access to accurate change management information and processes.

3.3.4 Availability management (SD 4.4) ✔

3.3.4.1 Purpose and objectives (SD 4.4.1) ✔

Availability management ensures that the level of availability delivered in all IT services meets the agreed availability needs in a cost-effective and timely manner. It is concerned with meeting both the current and future availability needs of the business.

The objectives of availability management are to:

- Produce and maintain the availability plan, reflecting the current and future needs of the business, and to provide guidance to the business and IT on availability-related issues
- Ensure that availability achievements meet or exceed targets and, where they do not, assist with the diagnosis and resolution of related incidents and problems
- Assess all changes for their impact on the availability plan and proactively improve availability, where cost-justifiable to do so.

3.3.4.2 Scope (SD 4.4.2) ✔

Availability management covers the design, implementation, measurement, management and improvement of IT service and component availability. It commences as soon as the availability requirements are clear and is an ongoing process, finishing only when the IT service is decommissioned or retired.

3.3.4.3 Value to business (SD 4.4.3) ✗

Service availability is at the core of customer satisfaction and business success. Customer dissatisfaction with the availability of services can be a key factor in losing business to a competitor.

Availability management ensures that the availability of services matches current and future business needs, and that the business impact of any unavailability is minimized.

3.3.4.4 Principles and basic concepts (SD 4.4.4) ✔

> **Definition: availability** ✔
>
> Ability of an IT service or other configuration item to perform its agreed function when required. Availability is determined by reliability, maintainability, serviceability, performance and security. Availability is usually calculated as a percentage. This calculation is often based on agreed service time and downtime. It is best practice to calculate availability of an IT service using measurements of the business output.

Availability management is completed at two interconnected levels:

- **Component availability** Involves all aspects of component availability
- **Service availability** Involves all aspects of service availability and the actual, or potential, service impact of component availability.

Availability management focuses on the following key aspects, which influence the overall availability and the business perception of unavailability:

- **Availability** The ability to perform an agreed function when required
- **Reliability** How long an agreed function can be performed without interruption
- **Maintainability** How quickly and effectively agreed functionality can be returned after a failure

■ **Serviceability** The ability of a third-party supplier to meet the terms of its contract, including agreed levels of availability, reliability and maintainability for a supporting service or component.

Availability management identifies **vital business functions** (VBFs) and takes these into account when making design recommendations. These recommendations can include designing for:

■ **High availability** To minimize or mask the effect of IT component failure
■ **Fault tolerance** To continue to operate correctly after failure of a component part
■ **Continuous operation** To eliminate planned downtime of an IT service
■ **Continuous availability** To achieve 100% availability – no planned or unplanned downtime.

3.3.4.5   Process activities, methods and techniques (SD 4.4.5) ✗

The key activities for availability management are:

■ Monitor, measure, analyse, report and review service and component availability
■ Unavailability analysis: investigating all events, incidents and problems involving unavailability and instigating remedial action
■ Service failure analysis: identifying the underlying causes of service interruptions
■ Identify VBFs and designing for availability and recovery
■ Component failure impact analysis (CFIA), single point of failure (SPOF) and fault tree analysis (FTA)
■ Model to determine whether new components will meet stated requirements.

3.3.4.6   Triggers, inputs, outputs and interfaces (SD 4.4.6) ✗

Triggers
- New or changed business needs or services
- Service or component breaches, availability events or alerts
- Periodic activities such as reviewing, revising or reporting.

Inputs
- Business information from the organization's business strategy
- Business impact from BIAs or assessment of VBFs
- Service information from the service portfolio and the service catalogue
- Past performance from previous measurements, achievements and reports
- Change and release information from the change schedule, the release and assessment of all changes for impact on service availability
- Unavailability and failure information from incidents and problems.

Outputs
- The AMIS
- The availability plan for the proactive improvement of IT services and technology
- Availability and recovery design criteria and proposed service targets
- Availability, maintainability and reliability reports.

Interfaces
- **SLM** Availability management determines and validates availability targets.
- **Incident and problem management** Availability management assists in the resolution and in subsequent, cost-justifiable corrective actions.

- **Capacity management** Provides appropriate capacity to support resilience and overall service availability.
- **Change management** Joint creation of the projected service outage (PSO) document.

3.3.4.7 Critical success factors and key performance indicators (SD 4.4.8) ✗

Table 3.4 Examples of critical success factors and key performance indicators for availability management

Critical success factor	Key performance indicator
Manage availability and reliability of IT service	Percentage reduction in the unavailability of services and components
	Percentage increase in the reliability of services and components
Satisfy business needs for access to IT services	Percentage reduction in critical time failures, e.g. during peak business usage hours
	Percentage reduction in cost of unavailability
Availability of IT infrastructure and applications as documented in SLAs at optimum cost	Percentage reduction in the cost of unavailability
	Percentage improvement in the service delivery costs

Table 3.4 includes some sample CSFs for availability management, followed by a small number of typical KPIs that support each CSF. Achievement against KPIs should be monitored and used to identify opportunities for improvement, which should be logged in the CSI register for evaluation and possible implementation.

3.3.4.8 Challenges and risks (SD 4.4.9) ✗

Challenges

- Meeting the high expectations of the business relating to the availability of services, including any assumptions based on 100% availability as an entry point and also on rapid recovery following a failure
- The ability to successfully gather and combine the huge amount of data available into a useful and integrated AMIS.

Risks

- Lack of commitment from the business to the availability management process
- Lack of senior management commitment or lack of resources
- Labour-intensive reporting processes
- Too much focus on the technology and not on the services or the needs of the business.

3.3.5 Information security management (SD 4.7) ✓

3.3.5.1 Purpose and objectives (SD 4.7.1) ✓

Information security management (ISM) is a governance activity within the corporate governance framework. It provides the strategic direction and is the focal point for all security activities. It ensures the objectives are achieved, that information security risks are managed and that enterprise information resources are used responsibly.

The purpose of ISM is to align IT security with business security and to ensure it matches the agreed needs of the business.

The objective is to protect the interests of those relying on information, and the systems and communications that deliver the information, from harm as a result of failures of confidentiality, integrity and availability.

3.3.5.2   Scope (SD 4.7.2) ✔

The term 'information' includes data stores, databases and metadata and takes into account all channels used to exchange or disclose that information.

ISM needs to understand:

- Business security policy and plans
- Current business operation and its security requirements
- Future business plans and requirements
- Legislative requirements
- Obligations and responsibilities with regard to security contained within SLAs
- Business and IT risks and their management.

ISM raises awareness across the organization of the need to secure all information assets.

3.3.5.3   Value to business (SD 4.7.3) ✗

ISM ensures that an information security policy is maintained and enforced that fulfils the needs of the business security policy and the requirements of corporate governance.

3.3.5.4   Principles and basic concepts (SD 4.7.4) ✔

Information security policy ✔

The information security policy should have the full support and commitment of top executive IT and business management, covering all areas of information security and appropriate to meet the ISM objectives.

Risk assessment and management ✗

Formal risk assessment and management relating to security of information and information processing is fundamental. ISM frequently collaborates with the business, ITSCM and availability management to conduct risk assessments.

Information security management system (ISMS) ✗

The ISMS is the basis for the development of a cost-effective information security programme that supports the business objectives. It is focused around five key elements, as indicated in Figure 3.3.

ISO/IEC 27001 is the formal standard against which organizations may seek independent certification of their ISMS.

3.3.5.5   Process activities, methods and techniques (SD 4.7.5) ✗

The key activities of ISM are:

- Produce, review and revise the information security policy
- Communicate, implement and enforce the security policies
- Assess and classify all information assets and documentation
- Implement and improve a set of security controls and risk responses

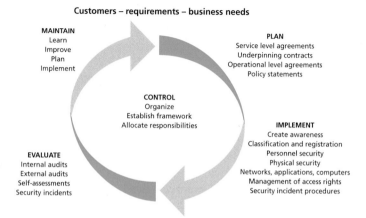

Figure 3.3 Elements of an information security management system for managing IT security

- Monitor and manage all security breaches and major security incidents
- Analyse, report on and take actions to reduce the volumes and impact of security incidents
- Schedule and complete security reviews, audits and penetration tests.

3.3.5.6   Triggers, inputs, outputs and interfaces (SD 4.7.6)

Triggers

- New or changed corporate governance guidelines
- New or changed business security policy
- New or changed business needs or services
- Service or component security breaches.

Inputs
- Business information from the organization's business strategy
- Governance and security from corporate governance and business security policies
- Details of security events and breaches
- Risk assessment processes and reports.

Outputs
- The information security policy
- An SMIS
- A set of security controls
- Security audits and audit reports.

Interfaces
- **SLM** Provides assistance with determining security requirements and responsibilities.
- **Access management** Performs the actions to grant and revoke access and applies the relevant policies.
- **Change management** ISM assists with the assessment of every change for impact on security.
- **Incident and problem management** ISM assists in the resolution of security incidents and problems, and in subsequent cost-justifiable corrective actions.
- **ITSCM** Collaborates on the assessment of business impact and risk.

3.3.5.7 Critical success factors and key performance indicators (SD 4.7.8)

Table 3.5 includes some sample CSFs for ISM, followed by a small number of typical KPIs that support each CSF. Achievement against KPIs should be monitored and used to identify opportunities for improvement, which should be logged in the CSI register for evaluation and possible implementation.

Table 3.5 Examples of critical success factors and key performance indicators for information security management

Critical success factor	Key performance indicator
Business is protected against security violations	Percentage decrease in security breaches
The determination of a clear and agreed policy, integrated with the needs of the business	Decrease in the number of non-conformances of the information security policy with the business security policy
Security processes that are justified, appropriate and supported by senior management	Increase in the acceptance of, and conformance to, security procedures
Effective marketing and education in security requirements	Increased awareness of the information security policy throughout the organization

3.3.5.8 Challenges and risks (SD 4.7.9)

Challenges

■ Ensuring adequate support for the information security policy from the business – information security objectives cannot be met without visible support and endorsement from business top management.

Risks

■ Lack of commitment from the business to the ISM process
■ Lack of senior management commitment or lack of resources or budget for the process

■ Risk assessment being conducted in isolation, not in conjunction with availability management and ITSCM.

3.3.6   Supplier management (SD 4.8) ✔

3.3.6.1   Purpose and objectives (SD 4.8.1) ✔

The purpose of supplier management is to obtain value for money from suppliers and to provide seamless quality of service to the business.

The objectives of supplier management are to:

■ Obtain value for money from all suppliers and contracts
■ Ensure that underpinning contracts (UCs) and agreements with suppliers are aligned with business needs, and support and align with agreed targets
■ Manage supplier performance and relationships with the suppliers
■ Negotiate and agree contracts with suppliers and manage them throughout their lifecycle
■ Maintain a supplier policy and a supporting supplier and contract management information system (SCMIS).

3.3.6.2   Scope (SD 4.8.2) ✔

The supplier management process includes the management of all suppliers and contracts needed to support the IT services. The process recognizes the supplier's value contribution and builds and manages a relationship that sustains that contribution. The relationship with each supplier is owned by an individual and is reviewed and managed centrally via the supplier management process.

3.3.6.3   Value to business (SD 4.8.3) ✗

Typically, suppliers are involved in some stage of the delivery of an end-to-end service. Where an external business partner or supplier is used, the SLA is supported by a UC.

The supplier management process ensures that all underpinning services supplied externally are appropriate to support the agreed targets and business needs laid out in the SLAs. This ensures delivery of a seamless, end-to-end service to the business.

3.3.6.4   Principles and basic concepts (SD 4.8.4) ✓

> **Definition: contract** ✗
>
> A contract is a legally binding agreement between two or more parties.

Supplier and contract management information system (SCMIS) ✗

In order to achieve consistency and effectiveness in the implementation of the supplier policy, an SCMIS should be established. It should record:

- All supplier and contract details
- Types of service or product provided by each supplier
- Relationships with other CIs.

Supplier categorization (SD 4.8.5.3) ✓

Managers should spend more time and effort managing key suppliers than less important suppliers. Suppliers can be categorized based on:

- Assessing the risk and impact associated with using the supplier
- The value and importance of the supplier and its services to the business.

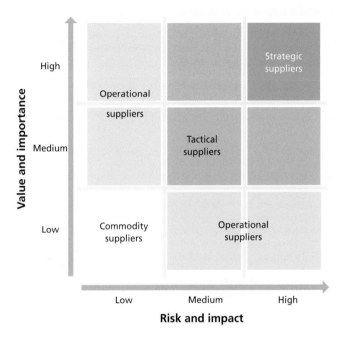

Figure 3.4 Supplier categorization

Figure 3.4 illustrates how to categorize suppliers.

The time and effort spent can then be appropriate to the supplier's categorization:

■ **Strategic** For significant 'partnering' relationships that involve senior managers sharing confidential strategic information to facilitate long-term plans

- **Tactical** For relationships involving significant commercial activity and business interaction
- **Operational** For suppliers of operational products or services
- **Commodity** For suppliers providing low value and/or readily available products or services.

3.3.6.5 Process activities, methods and techniques (SD 4.8.5) ✗

The activities of supplier management can be summarized in this way:

- Definition of new supplier and contract requirements
- Evaluation of new suppliers and contracts
- Supplier and contract categorization and maintenance of the SCMIS
- Establishment of new suppliers and contracts
- Supplier, contract and performance management
- Contract renewal or termination.

3.3.6.6 Triggers, inputs, outputs and interfaces (SD 4.8.6) ✗

Triggers

- New or changed corporate governance guidelines
- New or changed business strategies, needs or new or changed services
- Requirements for new contracts
- Re-categorization of suppliers.

Inputs

- Business information from the organization's business strategy
- Supplier and contracts strategy
- Supplier plans and strategies
- Suppler contracts, agreements and targets
- Supplier and contract performance information.

Outputs
- SCMIS
- Supplier and contract performance information and reports
- Supplier and contract review meeting minutes
- Supplier SIPs.

Interfaces
- **SLM** Provides assistance with determining targets.
- **Change management** Supplier contracts and agreements are controlled documents and therefore subject to the appropriate change management procedures.

3.3.6.7 Critical success factors and key performance indicators (SD 4.8.8) ✗

Table 3.6 Examples of critical success factors and key performance indicators for supplier management

Critical success factor	Key performance indicator
Business protected from poor supplier performance or disruption	Increase in the number of suppliers meeting the targets within the contract
Supporting services and their targets align with business needs and targets	Increase in the number of supplier and contractual targets aligned with the SLA and SLR targets
Availability of services is not compromised by supplier performance	Reduction in the number of service breaches caused by suppliers
Clear ownership and awareness of supplier and contractual issues	Increase in the number of suppliers with nominated supplier managers

Table 3.6 includes some sample CSFs for supplier management, followed by a small number of typical KPIs that support each CSF. Achievement against KPIs should be monitored and used to identify opportunities for improvement, which should be logged in the CSI register for evaluation and possible implementation.

3.3.6.8 Challenges and risks (SD 4.8.9) ✗

Challenges

- Working within an imposed, non-ideal contract that has poorly defined terms and conditions
- Insufficient expertise retained in the organization
- Losing the strategic perspective, focusing on operational issues, causing a lack of focus on strategic relationship objectives.

Risks

- Lack of commitment from the business and senior management to the supplier management process
- Legacy of badly written and agreed contracts that do not underpin or support business needs or SLA and SLR targets
- Supplier personnel or organizational culture not aligned with that of the service provider or the business.

3.3.7 Capacity management (SD 4.5) ✔

3.3.7.1 Purpose and objectives (SD 4.5.1) ✔

The purpose of capacity management is to ensure that the capacity of IT services and the IT infrastructure meets the agreed capacity and performance-related requirements in a cost-effective and timely manner.

The objectives of capacity management are:

■ Produce and maintain an accurate capacity plan, and provide advice and guidance on all capacity and performance-related issues

■ Ensure service performance achievements meet their agreed targets, and assist with diagnosis and resolution of incidents and problems

■ Assess the impact of all changes on the capacity plan and proactively improve performance, where cost-effective.

3.3.7.2   Scope (SD 4.5.2) ✔

Capacity management is a process that extends across the whole service lifecycle. A key factor in managing capacity is ensuring it is considered in service design. The capacity management process provides a focal point for the management of all IT performance and capacity issues.

Capacity management seeks to understand current and future business and IT needs relating to capacity and performance, and also to understand and take account of current capability and future opportunities presented by advances in technology.

Capacity management ensures that IT resources are planned and scheduled to deliver a consistent level of service, matched to the agreed current and future needs of the business.

3.3.7.3   Value to business (SD 4.5.3) ✘

Capacity management benefits the business through:

■ Improved performance and availability of IT services and reducing capacity- and performance-related incidents and problems

■ Ensuring required capacity and performance are provided in the most cost-effective manner

- Improving the reliability of capacity-related budgeting through the use of a forward-looking capacity plan.

3.3.7.4   Principles and basic concepts (SD 4.5.4) ✔

Capacity management is essentially a balancing act:

- Balancing costs against resources needed
- Balancing supply against demand.

Capacity management is a complex and demanding process. To deliver results it relies on three sub-processes:

- **Business capacity management** Translating business needs and plans into requirements for IT services and infrastructure
- **Service capacity management** Predicting, managing and controlling the end-to-end performance of the operational IT services and their workloads
- **Component capacity management** Predicting, managing and controlling the performance, utilization and capacity of individual IT components.

A capacity plan is used to manage the resources required to deliver IT services. The plan contains details of current and historic usage of IT services and components; plans for the development of IT capacity to meet the needs in the growth of both existing services; any agreed new services and any issues that need to be addressed (including related improvement activities). The plan also contains scenarios for different predictions of business demand and costed options to deliver the agreed service level targets.

3.3.7.5   Process activities, methods and techniques (SD 4.5.5) ✖

The main activities involved in the capacity management process are carried out in both a reactive and a proactive way. Generally, the more emphasis that is placed on proactive capacity management, the less effort that is required in reacting to incidents and problems due to capacity or performance-related issues.

The proactive activities of capacity management should include:

- Pre-empting performance issues by taking the necessary actions before they occur
- Producing trends of current utilization and estimating the future requirements
- Modelling and trending the predicted changes in IT services
- Ensuring that upgrades are budgeted, planned and implemented in a timely fashion
- Producing and maintaining a capacity plan
- Tuning (optimizing) the performance of services and components.

The reactive activities of capacity management should include:

- Monitoring, measuring, reporting and reviewing the current performance
- Responding to all capacity-related 'threshold' events and instigating corrective action
- Reacting to and assisting with specific performance issues.

3.3.7.6   Triggers, inputs, outputs and interfaces (SD 4.5.6) ✖

Triggers

- New and changed services requiring additional capacity
- Service breaches, capacity or performance events and alerts, including 'threshold' events.

Inputs

■ Business information from the organization's business strategy
■ Service and IT information from the service strategy and the IT strategy
■ Component performance and capacity information
■ Service performance issue information.

Outputs

■ CMIS containing information required by the sub-processes within capacity management
■ Capacity plan
■ Service performance information and reports.

Interfaces

■ **Availability management** Works with capacity management to determine the resources needed to ensure the required availability of services and components.
■ **SLM** Provides assistance with determining capacity targets.
■ **ITSCM** Assists with the assessment of business impact and risk and determining the capacity needed to support risk reduction measures and recovery options.

3.3.7.7 Critical success factors and key performance indicators (SD 4.5.8)

Table 3.7 includes some sample CSFs for capacity management, followed by a small number of typical KPIs that support each CSF. Achievement against KPIs should be monitored and used to identify opportunities for improvement, which should be logged in the CSI register for evaluation and possible implementation.

Table 3.7 Examples of critical success factors and key performance indicators for capacity management

Critical success factor	Key performance indicator
Accurate business forecasts	Percentage accuracy of forecasts of business trends
Knowledge of current and future technologies	Timely justification and implementation of new technology in line with business requirements
Ability to demonstrate cost-effectiveness	Reduction in the business disruption caused by a lack of adequate IT capacity
Ability to plan and implement the appropriate IT capacity to match the business need	Percentage reduction in the number of SLA breaches due to poor service or component performance

3.3.7.8   Challenges and risks (SD 4.5.9)

Challenges

- Ensuring the provision of accurate business plans on which to base the capacity plan
- Gathering and combining the huge amount of data available in a way that supports the capacity management process.

Risks

- Lack of commitment from the business to the capacity management process
- A lack of senior management commitment or a lack of resources and budget

■ Service and component capacity management performed in isolation because business capacity management is difficult
■ Bureaucratic or manually intensive processes.

3.3.8   IT service continuity management (SD 4.6) ✔

3.3.8.1   Purpose and objectives (SD 4.6.1) ✔

The purpose of IT service continuity management (ITSCM) is to support the overall business continuity management (BCM) process by ensuring that the IT service provider can always provide minimum agreed business continuity related service levels.

The objectives of ITSCM are to:

■ Maintain a set of IT service continuity plans and IT recovery plans that support the overall business continuity plans (BCPs) and, in support of this, to carry out regular BIA, risk analysis and management activities
■ Provide advice and guidance on continuity and recovery-related issues
■ Ensure that appropriate continuity mechanisms are in place to meet or exceed the agreed business continuity targets
■ Assess the impact of all changes on the IT service continuity plans
■ Ensure that proactive measures to improve the availability of services are implemented wherever it is cost-justifiable
■ Negotiate and agree contracts with suppliers for the provision of the necessary recovery capability.

3.3.8.2   Scope (SD 4.6.2) ✔

ITSCM serves to underpin the activities of the BCM process and focuses on those events that the business considers to be a 'disaster'. It does not cover minor technical faults which are addressed through the incident management process. These 'minor' issues are also covered by the availability management process in the design of services for availability and recovery.

Additionally, ITSCM does not usually directly address longer-term risks such as those from changes in business direction, diversification and restructuring, when there is generally time to evaluate the risks and address them through an IT change management programme.

3.3.8.3   Value to business (SD 4.6.3) ✗

ITSCM is invaluable in supporting the business strategy, as it is driven by business risk as identified by business continuity planning and ensures that recovery arrangements for IT services are aligned to business needs.

3.3.8.4   Principles and basic concepts (SD 4.6.4) ✔

Business continuity plan (BCP) ✗

A business continuity plan defines the steps required to restore business processes following a disruption. It also identifies triggers for invocation, people to be involved, communications etc. IT service continuity plans form a significant part of BCPs.

Business continuity management (BCM) ✗

BCM is responsible for managing risks that may seriously impact the business by reducing them to an acceptable level and then planning for the recovery of business processes should a business disruption occur. BCM sets the objectives, scope and requirements for ITSCM.

Business impact analysis (BIA) (SD 4.6.5.2) ✔

The purpose of BIA is to quantify the impact to the business that loss of service would have. It identifies:

- The form that the damage or loss may take
- How the degree of loss or damage is likely to escalate after a service disruption
- The staffing, skills, facilities and services (including the IT services) necessary to enable critical and essential business processes to continue operating at a minimum acceptable level
- The time within which minimum levels of staffing, facilities and services should be recovered
- The relative business recovery priority for each of the IT services.

Risk assessment (SD 4.6.5.2) ✔

This is an assessment of the level of threat and the extent to which the organization is vulnerable to that threat.

3.3.8.5   Process activities, methods and techniques (SD 4.6.5) ✘

A lifecycle approach should be adopted in setting up and operating ITSCM. The stages of the lifecycle form the foundation for the ITSCM activities, and, as illustrated in Figure 3.5, these are:

- Initiation
- Requirements and strategy
- Implementation
- Ongoing operation.

ITSCM is a cyclical process that ensures continuity and recovery plans exist and that they are continually aligned with the BCPs and business priorities. ITSCM should support the strategy and plans produced as a result of a BCM process.

Figure 3.5 Lifecycle of IT service continuity management

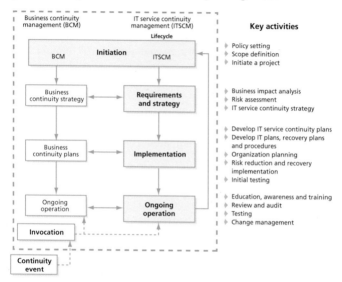

3.3.8.6   Triggers, inputs, outputs and interfaces (SD 4.6.6)

Triggers

- New or changed business needs or services
- New or changed targets within agreements
- The occurrence of a major incident that requires assessment for potential invocation of either business or IT continuity plans
- Periodic activities such as the BIA or risk assessment activities.

Inputs
- Business information from the organization's business strategy
- IT information from the IT strategy and plans
- Business continuity strategy and plans
- Change schedule and assess all changes for their impact on all ITSCM plans.

Outputs
- Revised ITSCM policy and strategy
- A set of ITSCM plans
- BIA exercises and reports
- Risks assessment and management reviews and reports
- ITSCM testing schedule.

Interfaces
- **Change management** All changes need to be assessed for their impact on the continuity plans.
- **Incident and problem management** Clear criteria need to be agreed for the invocation of the ITSCM plans.
- **Availability management** Undertaking risk assessment and implementing risk responses should be closely coordinated with the availability process to optimize risk mitigation.
- **SLM** Recovery requirements are agreed and documented in the SLAs.

3.3.8.7 Critical success factors and key performance indicators (SD 4.6.8) ✗

Table 3.8 includes some sample CSFs for ITSCM, followed by a small number of typical KPIs that support each CSF. Achievement against KPIs should be monitored and used to identify opportunities for improvement, which should be logged in the CSI register for evaluation and possible implementation.

Table 3.8 Examples of critical success factors and key performance indicators for IT service continuity management

Critical success factor	Key performance indicator
IT services are delivered and can be recovered to meet business objectives	Increase in success of regular audits of ITSCM plans to ensure that, at all times, the agreed recovery requirements of the business can be achieved
	Overall reduction in the risk and impact of possible failure of IT services
Awareness throughout the organization of the business and IT service continuity plans	Increase in validated awareness of business impact, needs and requirements throughout IT

3.3.8.8 Challenges and risks (SD 4.6.9) ✗

Challenges

- Developing appropriate ITSCM plans where there is no overall BCM process or plan. In such cases it is usually necessary for IT to educate the business to adopt best practice in this area
- Where IT plans are developed in the absence of business plans they may be inappropriate, and the blame for failure, in the event of a disaster, will be placed on IT.

Risks

- Lack of a BCM process
- Lack of commitment from the business to the ITSCM process
- Lack of appropriate information on future business plans and strategies

■ ITSCM plans and information become out of date and lose alignment with the information and plans of the business and BCM.

3.4   SERVICE DESIGN TECHNOLOGY-RELATED ACTIVITIES ✗

3.4.1   Requirements engineering (SD 5.1) ✗

Requirements engineering focuses on understanding and documenting the requirements of all stakeholders and on ensuring traceability of changes to each requirement.

There are three main types of requirement for any system:

■ **Functional** Describe the utility aspects of a service
■ **Management and operational** Describe the warranty aspects of a service
■ **Usability** Relate to how easy it is for the user to access and use the service.

A range of techniques may be used to investigate business situations and elicit service requirements, including:

■ Interviews
■ Workshops
■ Observation
■ Scenario analysis
■ Prototyping.

3.4.2   Management of data and information (SD 5.2) ✗

Data management is how an organization plans, collects, creates, organizes, uses, controls, disseminates and disposes of its data. It ensures the value of that data is identified and exploited. In this context data, as the basis for the organization's information, is treated as an asset.

The scope of data management includes four areas:

- ■ Management of data resources
- ■ Management of data/IT
- ■ Management of information processes
- ■ Management of data standards and policies.

3.4.3   Management of applications (SD 5.3) ✗

Definition: application ✗

An application is defined as software that provides functions which are required by an IT service. Each application may be part of more than one IT service. An application runs on one or more servers or clients.

An application is one component of the service, so it is important that it matches the agreed requirements of the business.

The application portfolio is a full record of all applications within the organization. There should be very close links between the service portfolio and the application portfolio.

3.5 TECHNOLOGY CONSIDERATIONS (SD 7) ✗

The use of service management tools is essential to the success of most process implementations. Tools requirements for processes across the lifecycle stages can be found in each of the core publications.

- ■ **Do** use tools to support and enhance (not replace) your assets, i.e. resources and capabilities
- ■ **Do** implement tools to support processes, not the other way around
- ■ **Do not** limit tools requirements to functionality
- ■ **Do not** assume purchasing a tool will solve all of your problems.

There are many tools and techniques that can be used to assist with the design of services by enabling:

- ■ Hardware and software design
- ■ Environmental design
- ■ Process design
- ■ Data design
- ■ Dashboards.

The automation of service processes can improve the utility and warranty of the service by:

- ■ Improving service quality
- ■ Reducing costs
- ■ Reducing complexity and uncertainty.

Selecting the right tool means paying attention to a number of issues:

- ■ An 80% fit to all functional requirements
- ■ Meeting all mandatory requirements
- ■ Little product customization required

- Adherence to service management best practice
- Integration with other service management and operations management tools
- Support of open standards and interfaces.

4   Service transition

ITIL Service Transition moves services and service changes into operational use. Service transition achieves this by receiving a new or changed service design package (SDP) from the service design stage, testing it to ensure it meets the needs of the business, and deploying it within the production environment.

ITIL Service Transition also introduces the service knowledge management system (SKMS), which can support organizational learning and help to improve the efficiency and effectiveness of all stages of the service lifecycle. This enables people to benefit from the knowledge and experience of others, support informed decision-making, and improve the management of services.

4.1   PURPOSE, OBJECTIVES, SCOPE AND VALUE OF SERVICE TRANSITION

4.1.1   Purpose and objectives (ST 1.1.1) ✔

The purpose of the service transition stage of the service lifecycle is to ensure that new, modified or retired services meet the expectations of the business as documented in the service strategy and service design stages of the lifecycle.

The objectives of service transition are to:

- Plan and manage service changes efficiently and effectively
- Manage risks relating to new, changed or retired services
- Successfully deploy service releases into supported environments
- Set expectations on the performance and use of new or changed services

- Ensure that service changes create the expected business value
- Provide knowledge and information about services and service assets.

4.1.2 Scope (ST 1.1.2) ✔

The scope of *ITIL Service Transition* includes the development and improvement of capabilities for transitioning new and changed services into supported environments, including release planning, building, testing, evaluation and deployment. The publication also considers service retirement and transfer of services between service providers.

4.1.3 Value to business (ST 1.1.4) ✔

Effective service transition provides the following benefits:

- Better estimation of cost, timing, resource requirement and risks
- Higher volumes of successful change
- Reduce delays from unexpected clashes and dependencies
- Reduced effort spent on managing test and pilot environments
- Improved expectation setting for all stakeholders
- Increased confidence that new or changed services can be delivered to specification without unexpectedly affecting other services or stakeholders
- Ensure that new or changed services will be maintainable and cost-effective
- Improved control of service assets and configurations.

4.2   KEY PRINCIPLES (ST 3.1) ✘

It is important to define and implement formal policies for service transition, for example:

- Implement all changes to services through service transition
- Adopt a common framework and standards
- Maximize re-use of established processes and systems
- Align service transition plans with the business needs
- Establish and maintain relationships with stakeholders
- Establish effective controls and disciplines
- Provide systems for knowledge transfer and decision support
- Plan release packages
- Anticipate and manage course corrections
- Proactively manage resources across service transitions
- Ensure early involvement in the service lifecycle
- Provide assurance of the quality of the new or changed service
- Proactively improve quality during service transition.

4.3   PROCESSES AND ACTIVITIES

4.3.1   Transition planning and support (ST 4.1) ✔

4.3.1.1   Purpose and objectives (ST 4.1.1) ✔

The purpose of the transition planning and support process is to provide overall planning for service transitions and to coordinate the resources that they require.

The objectives of transition planning and support are to:

- Plan and coordinate service transition resources within IT and across projects, suppliers and service teams where required
- Establish new or changed services within predicted cost, quality and time

- Establish new or modified management information systems and tools, technology and management architectures, service management processes, and measurement methods and metrics to meet agreed requirements
- Provide plans that enable business change projects to align with service transition
- Identify, manage and control risks
- Monitor and improve the performance of the service transition lifecycle stage.

4.3.1.2   Scope (ST 4.1.2) ✔

The scope of transition planning and support includes:

- Maintaining policies, standards and models for service transition
- Guiding major changes through service transition processes
- Prioritizing and coordinating resources needed to manage multiple transitions at the same time
- Planning service transition budget and resources
- Reviewing and improving the performance of transition planning and support.

Transition planning and support is not responsible for detailed planning for changes or releases.

4.3.1.3   Value to business (ST 4.1.3) ✗

Effective transition planning and support can significantly improve a service provider's ability to handle high volumes of change and releases across its customer base. An integrated approach to planning improves the alignment of the service transition plans with the customer, supplier and business change project plans.

4.3.1.4   Principles and basic concepts (ST 4.1.4) ✗
Service design coordination oversees the development of an SDP that documents each new or changed service. The SDP includes key information required by the service transition team, including:

- Expected utility and warranty
- Outline budgets and timescales
- Service specification
- Service models, architectural design, and detailed design of each release
- Release and deployment management plans
- Service acceptance criteria (SAC).

4.3.1.5   Process activities, methods and techniques (ST 4.1.5) ✗
Key activities for transition planning and support are:

- Defining the overall transition strategy, including policy, roles and responsibilities, standards and frameworks, success criteria
- Preparing for service transition, including the review and acceptance of inputs (e.g. SDP), raising requests for change (RFCs), checking transition readiness and baselining the configuration
- Planning and coordinating service transition, including production of service transition plans, reviewing and coordinating with release and deployment plans
- Providing transition process support, including advice, administration, progress monitoring and reporting.

4.3.1.6   Triggers, inputs, outputs and interfaces (ST 4.1.6) ✗
Triggers

- The trigger for planning a single transition is an authorized change

- Longer-term planning may be triggered by receipt of a change proposal from service portfolio management
- Budgeting for future transition requirements, triggered by the organization's budgetary planning cycle.

Inputs
- Change proposal
- Authorized change
- SDP.

Outputs
- Transition strategy and budget
- Integrated set of service transition plans.

Interfaces
- **Demand management** Provides information for longer-term planning.
- **Service portfolio management** Submits change proposals to trigger planning.
- **Business relationship management** Helps to manage communication with customers.
- **All service design processes** Contribute to the contents of SDPs.
- **All service transition processes** Are coordinated by transition planning and support. Pilots, handover and early life support must be coordinated with service operation functions.
- **Technical management and application management** Provide personnel, for example to review changes or plan deployments.
- **Project and programme management** Teams work very closely with transition planning and support.
- **Customers** Are involved in many aspects of service transition.

4.3.1.7   Critical success factors and key performance indicators (ST 4.1.8) ✗

Table 4.1 includes some sample critical success factors (CSFs) for transition planning and support, followed by a small number of typical key performance indicators (KPIs) that support each CSF. Achievement against KPIs should be monitored and used to identify opportunities for improvement, which should be logged in the CSI register for evaluation and possible implementation.

Table 4.1 Examples of critical success factors and key performance indicators for transition planning and support

Critical success factor	Key performance indicator
Understanding and managing trade-offs between cost, quality and time	Increase in number of releases that meet agreed requirements in terms of cost, quality, scope and time
	Reduced variation of actual versus predicted cost, quality, scope and time
Effective communication with stakeholders	Increased customer and user satisfaction
	Reduced business disruption due to better alignment between transition plans and business activities
Identifying and managing risks of failure and disruption	Reduction in number of issues, risks and delays
	Improved service transition success rates

Critical success factor	Key performance indicator
Coordinating activities of multiple processes involved in each transition	Improved efficiency and effectiveness of service transition processes
	Reduction in time and resource to develop and maintain integrated plans and coordination activities
Managing conflicting demands for shared resources	Increased project and service team satisfaction with service transition practices
	Reduced number of issues caused by conflicting demands for shared resources

4.3.1.8 Challenges and risks (ST 4.1.9)

Challenges

- Building up the relationships needed to manage and coordinate the many stakeholders who may be involved in service transition
- Coordinating and prioritizing many new or changed services, especially if there are delays or test failures that cause projects to slip.

Risks

- Lack of information from demand management and service portfolio management resulting in reactive transition planning and support with insufficient long-term planning
- Poor relationships with project and programme teams resulting in unexpected service transition requirements

- Delays to one transition having an effect on future transitions
- Insufficient information to prioritize conflicting requirements.

4.3.2 Change management (ST 4.2) ☑

4.3.2.1 Purpose and objectives (ST 4.2.1) ✓

The purpose of change management is to control the lifecycle of all changes, enabling beneficial changes to be made with minimum disruption to IT services.

The objectives of change management are to:

- Respond to changing business requirements while maximizing value and reducing incidents, disruption and re-work
- Respond to RFCs that will align services with business needs
- Ensure that changes are recorded and evaluated, and that authorized changes are prioritized, planned, tested, implemented, documented and reviewed in a controlled manner
- Optimize overall business risk.

4.3.2.2 Scope (ST 4.2.2) ✓

The scope of change management covers changes to all configuration items (CIs) across the whole service lifecycle, whether these CIs are physical assets such as servers or networks, virtual assets such as virtual servers or virtual storage, or other types of asset such as agreements or contracts. It also covers all changes to any of the five aspects of service design:

- Service solutions
- Management information systems and tools
- Technology architectures and management architectures
- Processes
- Measurement systems, methods and metrics.

Each organization should define their own scope, typically excluding business changes such as department reorganizations and operational changes such as a printer repair.

4.3.2.3   Value to business (ST 4.2.3) ✗

Change management enables the service provider to add value to the business by:

■ Protecting the business, and other services, while making required changes
■ Helping to meet governance, legal, contractual and regulatory requirements
■ Reducing unauthorized and failed changes and therefore service disruption
■ Contributing to better estimates of the quality, time and cost of change.

4.3.2.4   Principles and basic concepts (ST 4.2.4) ✔

Types of change request ✔

Changes are categorized as standard, emergency or normal changes:

■ **Standard change** A pre-authorized change that is low risk, relatively common and follows a procedure or work instruction – for example a password reset or provision of standard equipment to a new employee. RFCs are not required to implement a standard change, and they are logged and tracked using a different mechanism, such as a service request.
■ **Emergency change** A change that must be introduced as soon as possible, for example to resolve a major incident or implement a security patch. The change management process normally has a specific procedure for handling emergency changes.

- **Normal change** Any change that is not an emergency change or a standard change. Normal changes follow the defined steps of the change management process.

Changes are often categorized as major, significant and minor, depending on the level of cost and risk involved, and on the scope and relationship to other changes. This categorization may be used to identify an appropriate change authority.

Changes ✔, RFCs ✘ and change records ✘

The terms 'change', 'RFC' and 'change record' are often used inconsistently, leading to confusion. The usage in *ITIL Service Transition* is as follows:

- **Change** The addition, modification or removal of anything that could have an effect on IT services. The scope should include changes to all architectures, processes, tools, metrics and documentation, as well as changes to IT services and other CIs.
- **RFC** A request for change – a formal proposal for a change to be made. It includes details of the proposed change, and may be recorded on paper or electronically.
- **Change record** A record containing the details of a change throughout its lifecycle.

Change models ✔

A change model is a repeatable way of dealing with a particular category of change. It defines specific agreed steps that are followed for a change of this category. These models are often input to change management support tools that automate handling, management, reporting and escalation.

Each change model includes:

■ Steps that should be taken to handle the change, including escalation procedures for issues and unexpected events
■ Responsibilities for each step, including identification of change authorities
■ Timescales and thresholds for completion of actions.

Change models may be very complex with many steps that require authorization (e.g. major software release) or may be very simple with no requirement for authorization (e.g. password reset).

Change advisory board (CAB) ✔

A CAB is a group of people that supports the authorization of changes and assists change management in the assessment, prioritization and scheduling of changes. A CAB is often the change authority for one or more change categories, but in some organizations the CAB just plays an advisory role. In a large organization there may be many different CABs, with a global CAB responsible for the most significant changes and other CABs supporting different business units, geographies or technologies.

CABs should:

■ Be composed according to the changes being considered and vary in make-up even across the range of a single meeting
■ Involve suppliers when useful
■ Reflect both users' and customers' views
■ Include the problem manager, service level manager and customer relations staff for at least part of the time.

Emergency change advisory board (ECAB) ✔

For emergency change there may not be time to convene the full CAB, so it is necessary to identify a smaller board with authority to make emergency decisions – this is called an emergency change advisory board (ECAB).

Change procedures should specify how the composition of the CAB and ECAB is determined in each instance.

Change proposals ✔

Major changes that involve significant cost, risk or organizational impact are usually initiated through the service portfolio management process, and a change proposal is used to communicate a high-level description of the change. When the change proposal is authorized, the change schedule is updated to include outline implementation dates for the proposed change.

After the new or changed service is chartered, RFCs are used in the normal way to request authorization for specific changes. These RFCs are associated with the change proposal so that change management has a view of the overall strategic intent and can prioritize and review these RFCs appropriately.

Remediation planning ✔

No change should be authorized without a plan for what to do if it is not successful. Ideally, there is a back-out plan, but if the change is not reversible then an alternative approach is required. In some cases this may even require invoking the organization's business continuity plan.

Every change implementation plan should include milestones and other triggers for remediation to ensure there is sufficient time for this to occur.

Change schedule ✗

This schedule lists all approved changes and planned dates, as well as the estimated dates of longer-term changes. It is used to support processes such as incident and problem management, as well as being an important planning tool for change management.

4.3.2.5 Process activities, methods and techniques (ST 4.2.5) ✔

The key activities of change management are:

■ Planning, controlling and scheduling changes
■ Understanding the impact of change
■ Change decision making and change authorization
■ Change and release scheduling (working with release and deployment management)
■ Communication with stakeholders
■ Ensuring that there are remediation plans
■ Measurement, control and management reporting
■ Continual improvement.

Typical activities in managing individual changes are:

■ Create and record the RFC
■ Assess and evaluate the change:
  – Establish who should be involved in assessment and authorization
  – Evaluate the business justification, impact, cost, benefits and risks
■ Authorize the change if appropriate
■ Communicate the decision to all stakeholders, in particular the initiator of the RFC
■ Coordinate change implementation

■ Review and close the change, ensuring that lessons have been learned.

Figure 4.1 Example of a process flow for a normal change ✓

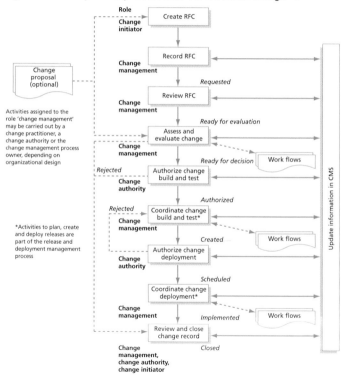

Each of these activities should store information in the SKMS and record it in the configuration management system (CMS), as appropriate. An example of a process flow for a normal change is shown in Figure 4.1.

4.3.2.6   Triggers ✗, inputs ✗, outputs ✗ and interfaces ✓ (ST 4.2.6)

Triggers

RFCs can be triggered throughout the service lifecycle and at the interfaces with other organizations, e.g. customers and suppliers. Other stakeholders, such as partners, may be involved with the change management processes, which may result in the submission of a change proposal, an RFC, or some other formal trigger to the change management process.

Inputs

- Policy and strategy for change and release
- RFC or change proposal
- Plans – change, transition, release, test, evaluation and remediation
- Current change schedule and projected service outage (PSO)
- Test results, test reports, evaluation reports and interim evaluation reports
- Configuration baseline.

Outputs

- Rejected and cancelled RFCs
- Authorized changes and change proposals
- Change to services or infrastructure resulting from authorized changes
- New, changed or disposed CIs
- Revised change schedule

- Authorized change plans
- Change documents, records and reports.

Interfaces

Change management must interface with almost all other service management processes:

- **Transition planning and support** Ensures there is a coordinated approach to managing service transitions.
- **Change evaluation and release and deployment management** Ensure that these processes work together to deliver the changes needed by the business.
- **Service asset and configuration management (SACM)** Provides access to configuration information needed to plan and evaluate changes, and updates the CMS as changes are implemented.
- **Service portfolio management** Submits change proposals before chartering new or changed services. Some change requests require analysis by service portfolio management, potentially adding to the service pipeline. Each organization should define criteria for deciding whether these requests are managed as part of the change management process or are passed to service portfolio management.

Some processes submit RFCs to both implement changes they need and to assess changes for impact on their areas of specialization, including:

- Problem management
- ITSCM
- Information security management (ISM)
- Capacity management and demand management.

Change management also has interfaces with areas outside of service management:

- With business programme and project management teams to ensure that change issues, aims, impacts and developments are communicated where appropriate.
- With programme and project management to ensure that the change schedule is effective and that all changes are well managed. Change management representatives may attend project or programme meetings.
- Some organizations have a function that manages organizational changes; in others this may be carried out within the IT organization. Change management must have appropriate interfaces with the people carrying out this work.

4.3.2.7 Critical success factors and key performance indicators (ST 4.2.8)

Table 4.2 includes some sample CSFs for change management, followed by a small number of typical KPIs that support each CSF. Achievement against KPIs should be monitored and used to identify opportunities for improvement, which should be logged in the CSI register for evaluation and possible implementation.

4.3.2.8 Challenges and risks (ST 4.2.9)

Challenges

- Ensuring that every change is recorded and managed
- Change management must make sure that it is seen to add value by helping changes happen faster and with higher success rates
- In some organizations, where change management only covers operational change authorization, migration to a true change management process that becomes involved early enough in the service lifecycle can be difficult

■ In large organizations there can be a significant challenge to agree and document the many levels of change authority that are needed to manage change effectively and to communicate effectively between these change authorities.

Table 4.2 Examples of critical success factors and key performance indicators for change management

Critical success factor	Key performance indicator
Responding to business and IT RFCs	Increase in percentage of changes that meet customer's agreed requirements
	Reduction in the backlog of change requests
	Increase in scores in survey of stakeholder satisfaction
Optimizing overall business risk	Reduction in percentage of emergency changes
	Increase in change success rate
	Reduction in the number of unauthorized changes identified
	Reduction in the number of incidents attributed to changes
Ensuring all changes to CIs are recorded and well managed	Reduction in number of audit compliance issues for change management
	Reduction in number of discrepancies found by SACM verification and audit

Risks

- Lack of commitment to the change management process by the business, IT management, and IT staff
- Implementation of changes without the use of change management
- Lack of clarity on how change management should interact with other service management processes, such as release and deployment management or SACM
- Excessively bureaucratic change management processes that introduce excessive delay to required changes.

4.3.3 Service asset and configuration management (ST 4.3) ✔

4.3.3.1 Purpose and objectives (ST 4.3.1) ✔

The purpose of the service asset and configuration management (SACM) process is to ensure that the assets required to deliver services are properly controlled, and that accurate and reliable information about those assets is available when and where it is needed. This information includes details of how the assets have been configured and the relationships between assets.

The objectives of SACM are to:

- Ensure that assets are identified, controlled, managed and protected throughout their lifecycle
- Identify, control, record, report, audit and verify services and other CIs, including their attributes and relationships
- Ensure the integrity of CIs and configurations by maintaining accurate configuration information on their historical, planned and current state in a CMS
- Support efficient and effective service management by providing accurate configuration information.

4.3.3.2   Scope (ST 4.3.2) ✓

Service assets that need to be managed in order to deliver services are known as configuration items (CIs). The scope of SACM includes management of the complete lifecycle of every CI. The scope also includes interfaces to internal and external service providers where there are assets and CIs that need to be controlled, e.g. shared assets.

Fixed asset management maintains an asset register, which records financial information about all of the organization's fixed assets. Fixed asset management is not usually under the control of the same business unit as the IT services, but the SACM process must provide proper care for the fixed assets under the control of IT.

4.3.3.3   Value to business (ST 4.3.3) ✗

Optimizing the performance of service assets and configurations improves the overall service performance and optimizes the costs and risks caused by poorly managed assets.

SACM provides visibility of accurate representations of a service, release or environment that enables:

- Better forecasting, assessment, planning and delivery of changes and releases
- Traceability of changes from requirements
- Resolution of incidents and problems within service level targets
- Delivery of service levels and warranties
- Better adherence to standards, legal and regulatory obligations
- More business opportunities as the service provider is able to demonstrate control of assets and services
- The ability to identify the costs of a service

■ Proper stewardship of fixed assets under the control of the service provider.

4.3.3.4   Principles and basic concepts (ST 4.3.4) ✔

Configuration items (CIs) ✔

It is important to distinguish between service assets, CIs and configuration records, as these concepts are often confused:

■ A **service asset** is any resource or capability that could contribute to the delivery of a service. Examples of service assets include a virtual server, a physical server, a software licence, or knowledge in the head of a manager.

■ A **configuration item** (CI) is any service asset that needs to be managed in order to deliver a service. All CIs are service assets, but many service assets are not CIs. Examples of CIs are a server or a software licence.

■ A **configuration record** is a set of attributes and relationships about a CI. Configuration records are stored in a configuration management database (CMDB) and managed with a CMS.

■ The **service knowledge management system** (SKMS) is a set of tools and databases that are used to manage knowledge, information and data. Many CIs are stored in the SKMS – for example, a service level agreement (SLA), a report template or a definitive media library (DML).

Configuration model ✘

A configuration model is a model of the services, assets and infrastructure, including relationships between CIs, that enables other processes to access valuable information (e.g. assessing the impact of incidents, problems and proposed changes; planning and designing new or changed services and their release and deployment; optimizing asset utilization and costs).

Configuration baseline ✗

A configuration baseline is the configuration of a service, product or infrastructure that has been formally reviewed and agreed upon, which thereafter serves as the basis for further activities and can be changed only through formal change procedures. A configuration baseline can be used as a checkpoint, a service development milestone, a basis for future builds and changes, to assemble components for a change or release or to provide the basis for a configuration audit or back-out.

Definition: configuration management system ✓

A set of tools, data and information that is used to support service asset and configuration management. The CMS is part of an overall service knowledge management system and includes tools for collecting, storing, managing, updating, analysing and presenting data about all configuration items and their relationships. The CMS may also include information about incidents, problems, known errors, changes and releases. The CMS is maintained by service asset and configuration management and is used by all IT service management processes.

Definition: definitive media library ✓

One or more locations in which the definitive and authorized versions of all software configuration items are securely stored. The definitive media library may also contain associated configuration items such as licences and documentation. It is a single logical storage area even if there are multiple locations. The definitive media library is controlled by service asset and configuration management and is recorded in the configuration management system.

4.3.3.5   Process activities, methods and techniques (ST 4.3.5)

The key activities of SACM are:

- **Management and planning** Deciding on the level of configuration management required for a service or a change project and creating a plan to achieve this.
- Configuration identification Defining CI types, naming conventions etc.
- **Configuration control** Ensuring there are adequate control mechanisms over CIs while maintaining a record of changes to CIs, versions, location and ownership.
- **Status accounting and reporting** Maintaining the status of CIs as they progress through their lifecycle. Examples of CI status could be Development, Approved, Withdrawn.
- **Verification and audit** Checking that the physical CIs exist, that documentation is accurate, and that all CIs are recorded in the CMS.

4.3.3.6   Triggers, inputs, outputs and interfaces (ST 4.3.6)

Triggers

- Updates from change management or release and deployment management
- Purchase orders or acquisitions
- Service requests.

Inputs

- Designs, plans and configurations from SDPs
- RFCs and work orders from change management
- Configuration information collected by tools and audits
- Information in the organization's fixed asset register.

Outputs

- New and updated configuration records
- Updated information for use in updating the fixed asset register

- Information about attributes and relationships of CIs
- Configuration snapshots and baselines
- Status reports, audit reports and other consolidated configuration information.

Interfaces

By its very nature – as the single virtual repository of configuration data and information for IT service management (ITSM) – SACM supports and interfaces with every other service management process and activity.

4.3.3.7 Critical success factors and key performance indicators (ST 4.3.8) ✗

Table 4.3 includes some sample CSFs for SACM, followed by a small number of typical KPIs that support each CSF. Achievement against KPIs should be monitored and used to identify opportunities for improvement, which should be logged in the CSI register for evaluation and possible implementation.

Table 4.3 Examples of critical success factors and key performance indicators for service asset and configuration management

Critical success factor	Key performance indicator
Accounting for, managing and protecting the integrity of CIs throughout the service lifecycle	Improved accuracy in budgets and charges for the assets utilized by each customer or business unit
	Reduced number of exceptions reported during configuration audits

Critical success factor	Key performance indicator
Supporting efficient and effective service management processes by providing accurate configuration information at the right time	Reduction in average time and cost of diagnosing and resolving incidents and problems
	Improved ratio of used licences against paid-for licences
	Reduction in risks due to early identification of unauthorized change
	Reduced percentage of changes not completed successfully or causing errors because of incorrect data in the CMS
Establishing and maintaining an accurate and complete CMS	Reduction in business impact of outages and incidents caused by poor SACM
	Improved audit compliance
	Fewer errors caused by people working with out-of-date information

4.3.3.8   Challenges and risks (ST 4.3.9)

Challenges

- Persuading technical support staff to adopt a checking in/out policy
- Attracting and justifying funding for SACM
- Lack of commitment and support from management.

Risks

- The temptation to consider it technically focused rather than service and business-focused
- Degradation of the accuracy of configuration information over time
- Setting the scope too wide, causing excessive cost and effort
- Setting the scope too narrow, so that the process has too little benefit.
- The CMS becomes out of date due to the movement of assets by non-authorized staff.

4.3.4 Release and deployment management (ST 4.4) ✔

4.3.4.1 Purpose and objectives (ST 4.4.1) ✔

The purpose of the release and deployment management process is to plan, schedule and control the build, test and deployment of releases, and to deliver new functionality required by the business while protecting the integrity of existing services.

The objectives of release and deployment management are to:

- Define and agree release and deployment management plans
- Create and test release packages, stored in a definitive media library (DML) and recorded in the CMS
- Deploy release packages from the DML following the agreed plan
- Ensure that organization and stakeholder change are managed
- Ensure that the new or changed service can deliver the agreed utility and warranty
- Ensure that there is knowledge transfer to customers, users and IT.

4.3.4.2 Scope (ST 4.4.2) ✔

The scope of release and deployment management includes the processes, systems and functions to package, build, test and deploy a release into live use, establish the service specified in the SDP, and formally hand the service over to the service operation functions.

The scope of release and deployment management does not include carrying out testing, or authorizing changes, but the process must ensure that these activities have been carried out.

4.3.4.3 Value to business (ST 4.4.3) ✘

Release and deployment management enables the service provider to add value to the business by:

■ Delivering change, faster and at optimum cost and minimized risk
■ Assuring that customers and users can use the new or changed service in a way that supports the business goals
■ Contributing to meeting auditable requirements for traceability.

Well planned and implemented release and deployment management can make a significant difference to an organization's service costs.

4.3.4.4 Principles and basic concepts (ST 4.4.4) ✔

Definition: release ✘

One or more changes to an IT service that are built, tested and deployed together. A single release may include changes to hardware, software, documentation, processes and other components.

Release policy ✔

Release and deployment management policies should be in place to help the organization achieve the correct balance between cost, service stability and agility.

For some services it is really important to maximize the stability of the service, even if this increases the amount of time required to design and test changes. For other services it may be more important to implement releases needed to support a rapidly changing business, and resources may be provided to ensure that this can be achieved.

Release identification ✗

All releases must be uniquely identified. The identification scheme needs to be described in the release policy, referencing the affected CIs, and including a version number.

Release unit ✗

A release unit is components of an IT service that are normally released together. A release unit typically includes sufficient components to perform a useful function.

Release package ✗

This describes one or more release units which are built, tested and deployed together as a single release.

Release deployment ✗

Deployments can either be big bang, i.e. all at once, or phased, i.e. deployed to users in stages and at different times.

A release can be 'pushed', whereby the service component is deployed from the centre and pushed out to the target; or 'pulled', whereby users are free to initiate the deployment when required. Mechanisms to release and deploy can be manual or automated.

4.3.4.5   Process activities, methods and techniques (ST 4.4.5) ✔

Figure 4.2 shows the four phases of release and deployment management:

- **Release and deployment planning** Plans for creating and deploying the release are created. This phase starts with change management authorization to plan a release and ends with change management authorization to create the release.
- **Release build and test** The release package is built, tested and checked into the DML. This phase starts with change management authorization to build the release and ends with change management authorization for the baselined release package to be checked into the DML. This phase only happens once for each release.
- **Deployment** The release package in the DML is deployed to the live environment. This phase starts with change management authorization to deploy the release package to one or more target environments and ends with handover to the service operation functions and early life support. There may be many separate deployment phases for each release.
- **Review and close** Experience and feedback are captured, performance targets and achievements are reviewed and lessons are learned.

Early-life support ✘

Once a new or changed service has been deployed into the production environment, service transition may provide early-life support for a limited period of time. During early-life support the service levels and monitoring thresholds are reviewed and additional resources may be provided for incident and problem management.

Figure 4.2 Phases of release and deployment management ✔

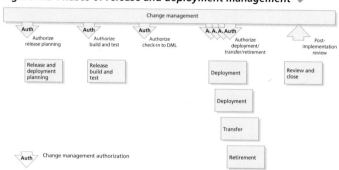

4.3.4.6   Triggers, inputs, outputs and interfaces (ST 4.4.6) ✗

Triggers

- Release and deployment management starts with receipt of an authorized change to plan, build and test a release package
- Deployment starts with receipt of an authorized change to deploy a release package to a target environment.

Inputs

- Authorized change
- SDP including a service charter, service models and SAC
- Acquired service assets and components and their documentation
- Environment requirements and specifications
- Release policy and release design
- Release and deployment models
- Exit and entry criteria for each stage of release and deployment.

Outputs
- New, changed or retired services
- New or changed documentation
- SLA, underpinning operational level agreements (OLAs) and contracts
- Release package checked in to DML and ready for future deployments
- CMS updates
- New or changed service reports
- Updated IT service continuity management (ITSCM) and capacity management plans.

Interfaces
- **Service design coordination** Creates the SDP that defines the new service, including all aspects of how it should be created. Release and deployment management also has a significant role to play in production of the SDP.
- **Transition planning and support** Provides the framework for release and deployment management to operate in, and transition plans provide the context for release and deployment plans.
- **Change management** Provides the authorization for the work that is carried out by release and deployment management, and release and deployment management provides the actual execution of many changes.
- **SACM** Release and deployment management depends on data and information in the CMS, and provides many updates to the CMS.
- **Service validation and testing** Release and deployment management must coordinate with service validation and testing, to ensure that testing is carried out when necessary, and that builds are available when required.

4.3.4.7   Critical success factors and key performance indicators (ST 4.4.8) ✗

Table 4.4 includes some sample CSFs for release and deployment management, followed by a small number of typical KPIs that support each CSF. Achievement against KPIs should be monitored and used to identify opportunities for improvement, which should be logged in the CSI register for evaluation and possible implementation.

Table 4.4 Examples of critical success factors and key performance indicators for release and deployment management

Critical success factor	Key performance indicator
Defining and agreeing release plans with customers and stakeholders	Increased number of releases that use a common framework of standards
	Increased number of releases that meet customer expectations for cost, time and quality
Ensuring integrity of a release package and its constituent components	Reduced number of deployments that do not use the DML
	Reduced number of incidents due to incorrect components being deployed

Critical success factor	Key performance indicator
Ensuring new or changed services can deliver agreed utility and warranty	Reduced variance from agreed service performance
	Increased customer and user satisfaction with the services
	Reduced resources to resolve incidents and problems
Ensuring that there is appropriate knowledge transfer	Reduced number of incidents categorized as 'user knowledge'
	Increased percentage of incidents solved by level 1 and level 2 support

4.3.4.8 Challenges and risks (ST 4.4.9)

Challenges

■ Developing standard performance measures and measurement methods across projects and suppliers
■ Dealing with projects and suppliers where estimated delivery dates are inaccurate and there are delays in scheduling service transition activities
■ Understanding the different stakeholder perspectives
■ Building a thorough understanding of risks and encouraging a risk management culture.

Risks

■ Poorly defined scope and understanding of dependencies
■ Using staff who are not dedicated to release and deployment management
■ Failing to use release and deployment management for service retirement

- Shortage of finances
- Organizational change affecting employee morale
- Failure of suppliers to meet contractual obligations.

4.3.5 Service validation and testing (ST 4.5) ✗

4.3.5.1 Purpose and objectives (ST 4.5.1) ✗

The purpose of the service validation and testing process is to ensure that a new or changed IT service matches its design specification and meets the needs of the business.

The objectives of service validation and testing are to:

- Provide confidence that a release will create a new or changed service that delivers the expected outcomes and value for the customers within the projected costs, capacity and constraints
- Validate that a service is 'fit for purpose' – it will deliver the required utility
- Provide assurance that a service is 'fit for use' – it will deliver the agreed warranty
- Confirm that customer and stakeholder requirements are correctly defined
- Identify, assess and address issues, errors and risks throughout service transition.

4.3.5.2 Scope (ST 4.5.2) ✗

Service validation and testing can be applied throughout the service lifecycle to quality assure any aspect of a service and the service providers' capability, resources and capacity to deliver a service and/or service release successfully.

Testing is equally applicable to in-house or developed services, hardware, software or knowledge-based services. It includes the testing of new or changed services or service components and examines the behaviour of these in the target business unit, service unit, deployment group or environment.

4.3.5.3 Value to business (ST 4.5.3) ✗

Key values to the business and customers from service testing and validation are, firstly, confidence that a new or changed service will deliver the value and outcomes required of it and, secondly, an understanding of the risks.

4.3.5.4 Principles and basic concepts (ST 4.5.4) ✗

Typical service validation and testing policy statements might include:

- All tests must be designed and carried out by people who have not been involved in other design or development activities for the service
- Test pass/fail criteria must be documented in a SDP before the start of any testing. Every test environment must be restored to a known state before testing is started
- Service validation and testing should create, catalogue and maintain a library of test models, test cases, test scripts and test data that can be re-used
- Adopt a risk-based testing approach aimed at reducing risk to the service and the customer's business.

Test models ✗

A test model includes a test plan, what is to be tested and the test scripts that define how each element will be tested. A test model ensures that testing is executed consistently in a repeatable way that is effective and efficient.

Figure 4.3 Example of a validation and testing process ✗

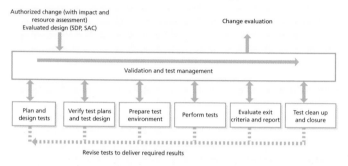

Revise tests to deliver required results

4.3.5.5 Process activities, methods and techniques (ST 4.5.5) ✗

The testing process is shown schematically in Figure 4.3. The test activities are not undertaken in a sequence. Several activities may be done in parallel, e.g. test execution can begin before all the test design is complete.

4.3.5.6 Triggers, inputs, outputs and interfaces (ST 4.5.6) ✗

Triggers

■ The trigger for testing is a scheduled activity on a release plan, test plan or quality assurance plan.

Inputs

■ An authorized change
■ An SDP, including the SAC.

Outputs
- Test report
- Updated data, information and knowledge to be added to the SKMS
- Test incidents, problems and error records
- Entries in the continual service improvement (CSI) register to address potential improvements.

Interfaces
- **Release and deployment management** Responsible for ensuring that appropriate testing takes place, but the actual testing is carried out as part of service validation and testing.
- **Change evaluation and change management** Require the outputs of service validation and testing as key inputs.
- **Service design coordination** Ensures that designs are testable and provides support for creating the SDP.

4.3.5.7 Critical success factors and key performance indicators (ST 4.5.8) ✗

Table 4.5 includes some sample CSFs for service validation and testing, followed by a small number of typical KPIs that support each CSF. Achievement against KPIs should be monitored and used to identify opportunities for improvement, which should be logged in the CSI register for evaluation and possible implementation.

4.3.5.8 Challenges and risks (ST 4.5.9) ✗

Challenges
- Lack of respect and understanding for the role of testing
- Lack of funding.

Table 4.5 Examples of critical success factors and key performance indicators for service validation and testing

Critical success factor	Key performance indicator
Building a thorough understanding of risks	Reduction in the impact of incidents and errors for newly transitioned services
	Increased number of risks identified in service design or early in service transition compared to those detected during or after testing
Encouraging a risk management culture	Increase in the number of people who identify risks
	Increase in the number of documented risks for each new or changed service
Developing re-usable test models	Increased number of tests in a repository for re-usable tests
	Increased number of times that tests are re-used
Achieving a balance between cost and effectiveness of testing	Reduced variance between test budget and test expenditure
	Reduced cost of fixing errors, due to earlier detection
	Reduction in business impact due to delays in testing

Risks

- Unclear expectations/objectives
- Lack of understanding of the risks resulting in testing that is not targeted at critical elements which need to be well controlled and therefore tested
- Resource shortages (e.g. users, support staff), which introduce delays and have an impact on other service transitions.

4.3.6 Change evaluation (ST 4.6) ✘

4.3.6.1 Purpose and objectives (ST 4.6.1) ✘

The purpose of change evaluation is to provide a consistent and standardized means of determining the performance of a service change in the context of likely impacts on business outcomes, and on existing and proposed services and IT infrastructure. The actual performance of a change is assessed against its predicted performance. Risks and issues related to the change are identified and managed.

The objectives of change evaluation are to:

- Set stakeholder expectations correctly
- Evaluate the intended effects of a service change and as much of the unintended effects as is reasonably practical
- Provide good-quality outputs so that change management can expedite an effective decision about whether or not a service change is to be authorized.

4.3.6.2 Scope (ST 4.6.2) ✘

Every change must be authorized at various points in its lifecycle; for example before build and test, before it is checked in to the DML and before it is deployed to the live environment. Evaluation is required before each of these authorizations, to provide the change authority with advice and guidance.

The change evaluation process describes a formal evaluation that is suitable for use when significant changes are being evaluated. Each organization must decide which changes should use this formal change evaluation, and which can be evaluated as part of the change management process.

4.3.6.3   Value to business (ST 4.6.3) ✗

Change evaluation establishes the use made of resources in terms of delivered benefit, and this information allows a more accurate focus on value in future service development and change management. There is a great deal of intelligence that CSI can take from change evaluation to inform future improvements to the process of change and the predictions and measurement of service change performance.

4.3.6.4   Principles and basic concepts (ST 4.6.4) ✗

As far as is reasonably practical, the unintended as well as the intended effects of a change need to be identified and their consequences understood.

The change evaluation process uses the Plan-Do-Check-Act (PDCA) model to ensure consistency across all evaluations. Each evaluation is planned and then carried out in multiple stages, the results of the evaluation are checked and actions are taken to resolve any issues found.

4.3.6.5   Process activities, methods and techniques (ST 4.6.5) ✗

The activities of the change evaluation process are illustrated in Figure 4.4.

Figure 4.4 Change evaluation process flow

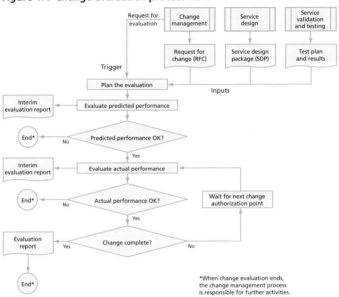

4.3.6.6 Triggers, inputs, outputs and interfaces (ST 4.6.6)

Triggers

■ The trigger for change evaluation is receipt of a request for evaluation from change management.

Inputs

■ SDP, including service charter and SAC
■ Change proposal, RFC, change record and detailed change documentation

- Discussions with stakeholders
- Test results and report.

Outputs

- Interim evaluation report(s) for change management
- Evaluation report for change management.

Interfaces

- **Transition planning and support** Works with change evaluation to ensure that appropriate resources are available.
- **Change management** Agreement on which types of change have formal evaluation, and process activities should be integrated with change evaluation.
- **Service design coordination** Informs change evaluation about the service in the form of an SDP.
- **Service level management (SLM) or business relationship management** Work with change evaluation to understand customer issues and obtain customer resources.
- **Service validation and test** Works with change evaluation and makes use of test results.

4.3.6.7 Critical success factors and key performance indicators (ST 4.6.8)

Table 4.6 includes some sample CSFs for change evaluation, followed by a small number of typical KPIs that support each CSF. Achievement against KPIs should be monitored and used to identify opportunities for improvement, which should be logged in the CSI register for evaluation and possible implementation.

Table 4.6 Examples of critical success factors and key performance indicators for change evaluation

Critical success factor	Key performance indicator
Stakeholders have a good understanding of the expected performance of new and changed services	Reduced number of incidents for new or changed services due to failure to deliver expected utility or warranty
	Increased stakeholder satisfaction with new or changed services as measured in customer surveys
Change management has good quality evaluations to help them make correct decisions	Increased percentage of evaluations delivered by agreed times
	Reduced number of changes that have to be backed out due to unexpected errors or failures
	Reduced number of failed changes

4.3.6.8   Challenges and risks (ST 4.6.9)

Challenges

- Developing standard performance measures and measurement methods across projects and suppliers
- Understanding the different stakeholder perspectives
- Understanding the balance between managing risk and taking risks, communicating the organization's attitude to risk and encouraging a risk management culture
- Building a thorough understanding of risks that have impacted or may impact transition of services.

Risks

- Lack of clear criteria for when change evaluation should be used
- Unrealistic expectations of the time required for change evaluation
- Personnel with insufficient experience or organizational authority to be able to influence change authorities
- Projects and suppliers causing delays in scheduling change evaluation.

4.3.7   Knowledge management (ST 4.7) ✔

4.3.7.1   Purpose and objectives (ST 4.7.1) ✔

The purpose of the knowledge management process is to share perspectives, ideas, experience and information; to ensure that these are available in the right place at the right time to enable informed decisions; and to improve efficiency by reducing the need to rediscover knowledge.

The objectives of knowledge management are to:

- Improve management decision-making by ensuring that reliable and secure knowledge, information and data are available
- Enable the service provider to be more efficient and improve quality of service, increase satisfaction and reduce the cost of service
- Maintain an SKMS that provides controlled access to appropriate knowledge, information and data
- Gather, analyse, store, share, use and maintain knowledge, information and data throughout the service provider organization.

4.3.7.2   Scope (ST 4.7.2) ✔

Knowledge management is a whole lifecycle-wide process in that it is relevant to all lifecycle stages and hence is referenced throughout ITIL from the perspective of each publication.

4.3.7.3   Value to business (ST 4.7.3) ✘

Successful management of data, information and knowledge delivers:

- Conformance with legal and other requirements
- Documented requirements for retention of each category of data, information and knowledge
- Data, information and knowledge that is current, complete and valid.

Effective knowledge management is a powerful asset for people in all roles across all stages of the service lifecycle.

4.3.7.4   Principles and basic concepts (ST 4.7.4) ✔

Data-to-Information-to-Knowledge-to-Wisdom (DIKW) (ST 4.7.4.2) ✔

Knowledge management uses the DIKW hierarchy to help create value, as illustrated in Figure 2.7.

Data is a set of discrete facts. An example of data is the date and time at which an incident was logged.

Information comes from providing context to data. An example of information is the average time to close priority 2 incidents.

Knowledge is composed of the tacit experiences, ideas, insights, values and judgements of individuals. An example of knowledge is that the average time to close priority 2 incidents has increased by about 10% since a new version of the service was released.

Wisdom makes use of knowledge to create value through correct and well-informed decisions. An example of wisdom is recognizing that the increase in time to close priority 2 incidents is due to poor-quality documentation for the new version of the service.

Service knowledge management system (SKMS) (ST 4.7.4.3) ✔

> **Definition: service knowledge management system** ✔
>
> A set of tools and databases that is used to manage knowledge, information and data. The service knowledge management system includes the configuration management system, as well as other databases and information systems. The service knowledge management system includes tools for collecting, storing, managing, updating, analysing and presenting all the knowledge, information and data that an IT service provider will need to manage the full lifecycle of IT services.

Figure 4.5 is a simplified illustration of the relationship of the SKMS, the CMS and the CMDB. The SKMS supports delivery of the services and informed decision-making, and is underpinned by the CMS, but it should also contain many other things, for example:

- The service portfolio
- The DML
- SLAs, contracts and OLAs
- The CSI register and service improvement plans (SIPs)
- The capacity plan and capacity management information system
- Project plans from previous projects
- Skills register, and typical and anticipated user skill levels
- Web-based training courses.

Figure 4.5 Relationship of the SKMS, the CMS and the CMDB ✔

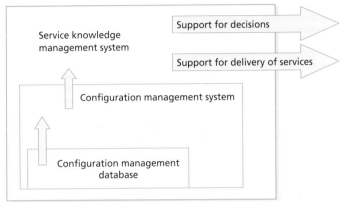

4.3.7.5   Process activities, methods and techniques (ST 4.7.5) ✗

The key activities of knowledge management are:

- **Define knowledge management strategy** An overall strategy is required including how to identify, capture and maintain knowledge.
- **Knowledge transfer** Retrieving and sharing knowledge in order to solve problems and support dynamic learning, strategic planning and decision making.
- **Evaluation and improvement** Measure the use made of the data, evaluate its usefulness, and identify improvements.

4.3.7.6   Triggers, inputs, outputs and interfaces (ST 4.7.6) ✗

Triggers

- Knowledge management has many triggers, relating to every requirement for storing, maintaining or using knowledge, information or data within the organization.

- Inputs to knowledge management include all knowledge, information and data used by the service provider, as well as relevant business data.

- The key output of knowledge management is the knowledge required to make decisions and to manage the IT services, maintained within an SKMS.

- Knowledge management has interfaces with every other service management process. The SKMS can only be effective if all processes use it to store and manage information and data.

4.3.7.7 Critical success factors and key performance indicators (ST 4.7.8) ✗

Table 4.7 includes some sample CSFs for knowledge management, followed by a small number of typical KPIs that support each CSF. Achievement against KPIs should be monitored and used to identify opportunities for improvement, which should be logged in the CSI register for evaluation and possible implementation.

4.3.7.8 Challenges and risks (ST 4.7.9) ✗

- Justifying the effort that would be needed to create a consistent architecture for managing existing stores of knowledge, information and data
- Ensuring all stakeholders understand the added value that a more holistic approach to knowledge management can bring, and to continue to demonstrate this value as an SKMS is built, where each group or team within the service provider owns and manages information that they use, and may see knowledge management as interfering in their work.

Table 4.7 Examples of critical success factors and key performance indicators for knowledge management

Critical success factor	Key performance indicator
Availability of knowledge and information that helps to support management decision-making	Increased number of accesses to the SKMS by managers
	Increased percentage of SKMS searches by managers that receive a rating of 'good'
Reduced time and effort required to support and maintain services	Increased number of times that material is re-used in documentation such as procedures, test design and service desk scripts
	Reduced transfer of issues to other people and more resolution at lower staff levels
	Increased percentage of incidents solved by use of known errors
Reduced dependency on personnel for knowledge	Increased number of times that the SKMS is accessed
	Increased percentage of SKMS searches that receive a rating of 'good' by the user
	Increased scores in regular customer satisfaction survey for knowledge management

Risks

- Focusing on the supporting tools, rather than on the creation of value
- Insufficient understanding of what knowledge, information and data are needed
- Spending too much effort on knowledge capture with insufficient attention to knowledge transfer and re-use
- Storing and sharing knowledge and information that are not up to date and relevant
- Lack of support and commitment from stakeholders.

4.4   MANAGING PEOPLE THROUGH SERVICE TRANSITIONS (ST 5) ✘

4.4.1   Managing communications and commitment (ST 5.1) ✘

Communication is central to any service transition. The greater the change, the greater the need for clear communication about the reasons and rationale behind it, the benefits expected, the plans for its implementation and its proposed effects. Communications need to be timely, targeted at the right audience and to clearly communicate the messages and benefits consistently.

4.4.2   Managing organization and stakeholder change (ST 5.2) ✘

The research on change management strongly suggests that without the support of people, change will not happen. Business managers and change agents must understand the emotional impact that change has on people and how to manage it accordingly.

Factors that drive successful change initiatives at the organization level include:

- Leadership for the change
- Organization adoption
- Governance
- Organization capabilities
- Business and service performance measures
- A strong communication process with regular opportunity for staff feedback.

Each organization and combination of organizations is different, so the service transition approach to change is determined, in part, by the culture and may vary across the organization.

4.5   TECHNOLOGY CONSIDERATIONS (ST 7) ✗

Some enterprise-wide tools support the broader systems and processes within which service transition delivers support. These include:

- ITSM systems that can integrate a CMS with tools to support specific service management processes
- System, network and application management tools
- Service dashboards and reporting tools.

Other tools are targeted more specifically at supporting service transition or parts of service transition:

- SKMS – this may be a tool used by the business as well as IT
- Configuration management systems and tools
- Version control tools
- Requirements management tools
- Tools for software distribution and installation
- Build and release tools
- Discovery and audit tools.

A wide variety of tools may be needed to support knowledge management, including:

- Document management and records management tools
- Content management tools
- Tools to support web publishing, wikis, blogs, word processing, data and financial analysis, presentation, flow charting, publication and distribution
- Collaboration tools such as shared calendars and tasks, threaded discussions, instant messaging, video conferencing and email.

When designing a CMS you should consider whether the following functionality is needed:

- Ability to integrate multiple data sources
- Security controls to limit access
- Hierarchical and networked relationships between CIs
- Automatic validation of input data (e.g. are all CI names unique?) and determination of relationships where possible
- Automatic identification of other affected CIs when any CI is the subject of an incident, problem, known error, change or release
- Maintenance of a history of all CIs
- Support for the management and use of configuration baselines
- Ease of interrogation of the CMS and good reporting facilities, including trend analysis, and ease of reporting to facilitate configuration audits and impact analyses
- The ability to show configuration models, maps and the hierarchy of relationships between CIs.

5   Service operation

Strategic objectives are ultimately realized through service operation, requiring effective and efficient delivery and support of IT services to ensure value for the customer and the service provider.

5.1   PURPOSE, OBJECTIVES, SCOPE AND VALUE OF SERVICE OPERATION

5.1.1   Purpose and objectives (SO 1.1.1) ✔

The purpose of the service operation stage of the service lifecycle is to coordinate and carry out the activities and processes required to deliver and manage services at agreed levels to business users and customers. Service operation is also responsible for the ongoing management of the technology that is used to deliver and support services.

Service operation is a critical stage of the service lifecycle. Well planned and well implemented processes are to no avail if the day-to-day operation of those processes is not properly conducted, controlled and managed. Nor will service improvements be possible if day-to-day activities to monitor performance, assess metrics and gather operational data are not systematically conducted during service operation.

The objectives of service operation are to:

■ Maintain business satisfaction and confidence in IT through effective and efficient delivery and support of agreed IT services

- Minimize the impact of service outages on day-to-day business activities
- Ensure that access to agreed IT services is only provided to those authorized to receive those services.

5.1.2 Scope (SO 1.1.2) ✔

Service operation describes the processes, functions, organization and tools used to underpin the ongoing activities required to deliver and support services and includes:

- **Services** Activities that form part of a service are included in service operation, whether it is performed by the service provider, an external supplier or the user or customer of that service.
- **Service management processes** The ongoing management and execution of the many service management processes that are performed in service operation. Even though a number of ITIL processes (such as change and capacity management) originate at the service design or service transition stage of the service lifecycle, they are in use continually in service operation.
- **Technology** All services require some form of technology to deliver them. Managing technology is an integral part of the management of the services.
- **People** People drive the demand for the organization's services and products; decide how this will be done; manage the technology, processes and services. Failure to recognize this will result (and has resulted) in the failure of service management activities.

5.1.3 Value to business (SO 1.1.4) ✔

Service operation is the stage in the lifecycle where the plans, designs and optimizations are executed and measured. Service operation is where actual value is seen by the business. Adopting and implementing standard and consistent approaches for service operation:

■ Reduces the duration and frequency of service outages, which will allow the business to take full advantage of the value created by the services they are receiving and reduce unplanned costs and resource usage

■ Provides operational results and data to provide justification for investing in ongoing service improvement activities and supporting technologies

■ Meets the goals and objectives of the organization's security policy by ensuring that IT services will be accessed only by those authorized to use them

■ Provides quick and effective access to standard services which business staff can use to improve their productivity or the quality of business services and products

■ Provides a basis for automated operations, thus increasing efficiencies and allowing expensive human resources to be used for more innovative work, such as designing new or improved functionality or defining new ways in which the business can exploit technology for increased competitive advantage.

5.2   KEY PRINCIPLES

5.2.1 Achieving balance in service operations (SO 3.2) ✘

Service operation has to achieve a balance between many conflicting requirements. Each of these conflicts represents an opportunity for the organization to grow and improve.

- **Internal IT view versus external business view** The external view is how the IT services are experienced by users and customers. The internal view is how the technology components and systems are managed to deliver the services. An organization that only focuses on business requirements may make promises that cannot be met. An organization that focuses on the internal view only may deliver expensive services with little value.

- **Stability versus responsiveness** An extreme focus on stability may result in business requirements being ignored, an extreme focus on responsiveness may result in unstable and unreliable IT services.

- **Quality of service versus cost of service** Service operation must deliver agreed levels of service whilst keeping costs low. Too much focus on cost may result in missing agreed service levels. Too much focus on quality may lead to overspending.

- **Reactive versus proactive** A reactive organization waits for events before it does anything. A proactive organization is always looking for ways to improve. An organization that is too reactive may be unable to support business strategy. An organization that is too proactive may fail to respond quickly enough to unpredicted events, resulting in customer dissatisfaction. They may also spend more than is needed on fixing things that are not impacting, leading to higher levels of change.

5.2.2   Communication in service operation (SO 3.6) ✔

Effective communication in service operation ensures that all teams and departments are able to execute the standard activities involved in delivering IT services and managing the IT infrastructure, including:

- **Routine operational communication** To coordinate the regular activities of service operation and ensure staff are aware of scheduled activities and any changes
- **Communication between shifts** To ensure that any handover between shifts is effective
- **Performance reporting** IT service performance and service operation team or department performance
- **Communication in projects** To manage communication between projects and the involvement of service operation staff
- **Communication related to changes** Information required to assess the impact of and successfully implement or back-out changes
- **Communication related to exceptions** Information around any occurrence that is outside expected activity or performance
- **Communication related to emergencies** To allow effective investigation and management of emergency situations
- **Communication with users and customers** A focus on customer or user requirements and concerns.

5.3   PROCESSES AND ACTIVITIES

5.3.1   Incident management (SO 4.2) ☑

5.3.1.1   Purpose and objectives (SO 4.2.1) ✓

The purpose of incident management is to restore normal service operation as quickly as possible and minimize the adverse impact on business operations, thus ensuring that agreed levels of service quality are maintained. 'Normal service operation' is defined as an operational state where services and configuration items (CIs) are performing within their agreed service and operational levels.

The objectives of the incident management process are to:

- Ensure that standardized methods and procedures are used for efficient and prompt response, analysis, documentation, ongoing management and reporting of incidents
- Increase visibility and communication of incidents to business and IT support staff
- Enhance business perception of IT through use of a professional approach in quickly resolving and communicating incidents when they occur
- Align incident management activities and priorities with those of the business
- Maintain user satisfaction with the quality of IT services.

5.3.1.2   Scope (SO 4.2.2) ✓

Incident management includes any event which disrupts, or which could disrupt, a service. This includes events which are communicated directly by users, either through the service desk, through an interface from event management to incident management tools or incidents reported and/or logged by technical staff. This does not mean, however, that all events are incidents. Many classes of events are not related to disruptions at all, but are indicators of normal operation or are simply informational (see section 5.3.3).

Although both incidents and service requests are reported to the service desk, this does not mean that they are the same. Service requests do not represent a disruption to agreed service, but are a way of meeting the customer's needs and may be addressing an agreed target in a service level agreement (SLA). Service requests are dealt with by the request fulfilment process.

5.3.1.3 Value to business (SO 4.2.3) ✗

The value of incident management includes the ability to:

- Reduce unplanned labour and costs for both the business and IT support staff
- Detect and resolve incidents resulting in lower downtime and higher service availability
- Identify business priorities and dynamically allocate resources to incidents based on real-time business priorities
- Identify potential improvements to services by understanding what constitutes an incident and aligning with the activities of business operational staff
- Identify additional service or training requirements found in IT or the business.

Incident management is highly visible to the business, and it is therefore easier to demonstrate its value than most areas in service operation. For this reason, incident management is often one of the first processes to be implemented in service management projects. The added benefit of doing this is that incident management can be used to highlight other areas that need attention – thereby providing a justification for expenditure on implementing other processes.

5.3.1.4   Principles and basic concepts (SO 4.2.4) ✔

Definition: incident ✔

An incident is an unplanned interruption to an IT service or reduction in the quality of an IT service. Failure of a configuration item that has not yet affected service is also an incident – for example, failure of one disk from a mirror set.

Definition: impact ✔

Impact is a measure of the effect of an incident, problem or change on business processes. Impact is often based on how service levels will be affected. Impact and urgency are used to assign priority.

Definition: urgency ✔

A measure of how long it will be until an incident, problem or change has a significant impact on the business. For example, a high-impact incident may have low urgency if the impact will not affect the business until the end of the financial year. Impact and urgency are used to assign priority.

Definition: priority ✔

A category used to identify the relative importance of an incident, problem or change. Priority is based on impact and urgency, and is used to identify required times for actions to be taken. For example, the service level agreement may state that Priority 2 incidents must be resolved within 12 hours.

Timescales ✔

Timescales must be agreed for all incident handling activities, based upon the overall incident response and resolution targets agreed within SLAs, operational level agreements (OLAs) and underpinning contracts (UCs). All support groups should be made fully aware of these timescales.

Incident models ✔

An incident model is a way of predefining the steps that should be taken to handle a particular type of incident in an agreed way. Support tools can then be used to manage the required process. This ensures that 'standard' incidents are handled in a predefined path and within predefined timescales.

Major incidents ✔

A major incident is often confused with a problem. In reality, an incident remains an incident for ever – it may grow in impact or priority to become a major incident, but an incident never 'becomes' a problem. A definition of what constitutes a major incident must be agreed so that they are dealt with through a separate major incident procedure. Where necessary this procedure should include the establishment of a separate major incident team under the leadership of the incident manager, to concentrate on this major incident alone to ensure that adequate resources and focus are used to find a speedy resolution.

Incident status and tracking ✔

Incidents should be tracked throughout their lifecycle to support proper handling and reporting on the status of incidents. Within the incident management system, status codes may be linked to incidents to indicate where they are in relation to the lifecycle. Examples include: open, in-progress, resolved and closed.

Expanded incident lifecycle ✔

The expanded incident lifecycle can be used to help understand all stages and activities involved in the incident lifecycle and their impact on the resolution of incidents and their subsequent improvement.

5.3.1.5 Process activities, methods and techniques (SO 4.2.5) ✔

The key activities for incident management are:

- **Incident identification** Incidents may be detected by event management, by calls to the service desk, from web or other self-help interfaces, or directly by technical staff.
- **Incident logging** All incidents must be logged and time-stamped, regardless of how they are received. The log must include sufficient data to enable the incident to be managed.
- **Incident categorization** Categories are used to identify the type of incident and to identify service requests so they can be passed to the request fulfilment process. Categories are also checked when the incident is closed
- **Incident prioritization** A priority code is assigned based on impact and urgency. Priorities are dynamic and may be changed during the life of the incident
- **Initial diagnosis** If possible, the incident should be resolved while the user is on the telephone. Sometimes the service desk analyst will continue to work on the incident and contact the user when it has been resolved
- **Incident escalation** 'Functional escalation' is transferring the incident to a technical team with a higher level of expertise; 'hierarchic escalation' is informing or involving more senior levels of management.
- **Investigation and diagnosis** All actions taken by support groups should be recorded in the incident record.

- **Resolution and recovery** The resolution must be fully tested and documented in the incident record, before the incident is passed back to the service desk for closure.
- **Incident closure** Check and confirm the incident categories, carry out a user satisfaction survey, ensure all incident documentation is up to date, check to see if a problem record should be raised and then close the incident with the appropriate closure categorization.
- **Rules for reopening incidents** Despite all adequate care, there will be occasions when incidents recur even though they have been formally closed. Because of such cases, it is wise to have predefined rules about if and when an incident can be reopened.

5.3.1.6 Triggers ✗, inputs ✗, outputs ✗ and interfaces ✔ (SO 4.2.6)

Triggers

- A user calls the service desk or completes a web-based log of an incident
- An incident is automatically raised via event management tools
- Technical staff may notice potential failures and raise an incident
- Incidents may be raised at the request of suppliers.

Inputs

- Information about CIs and their status
- Information about known errors and workarounds
- Communication about incidents and their symptoms
- Communication about requests for change (RFCs) and releases
- Communication of events
- Operational and service level objectives

- Customer feedback
- Agreed criteria for prioritizing and escalating incidents.

Outputs

- Resolved incidents and resolution actions
- Updated incident management records
- Problem records
- Feedback on incidents related to changes and releases
- Identification of CIs associated with or impacted by incidents
- Satisfaction feedback.

Interfaces

- **Service level management (SLM)** Requires a process capable of resolving incidents in a specified time which can also provide information and reports that enable SLM to review services and identify service weaknesses and improvements.
- **Information security management (ISM)** Requires information on security incidents to measure the effectiveness of security measures and support service design activities.
- **Capacity management** Requires performance monitoring and information on performance issues and problems.
- **Availability management** Requires information on the availability of IT services and the improvement of the incident lifecycle.
- **Service asset and configuration management (SACM)** Provides data to identify and progress incidents, identify faulty equipment and to assess the impact of an incident.
- **Change management** The implementation of a workaround or resolution is logged as an RFC and progressed through change management. Incident management needs to detect and resolve incidents arising from failed changes.
- **Problem management** Provides known errors and workarounds for faster incident resolution and also the

investigation and resolution of the underlying cause of incidents preventing or reducing the impact of recurrence.

■ **Access management** Requires information on unauthorized access attempts and security breaches.

5.3.1.7 Critical success factors and key performance indicators (SO 4.2.8)

Table 5.1 includes some sample critical success factors (CSFs) for incident management, followed by a small number of typical key performance indicators (KPIs) that support each CSF. Achievement against KPIs should be monitored and used to identify opportunities for improvement, which should be logged in the CSI register for evaluation and possible implementation.

Table 5.1 Examples of critical success factors and key performance indicators for incident management

Critical success factor	Key performance indicator
Resolve incidents as quickly as possible, minimizing impacts to the business	Mean elapsed time to achieve incident resolution or circumvention
	Breakdown of incidents at each stage
	Percentage of incidents closed by the service desk without referral to other support groups
	Number and percentage of incidents resolved remotely
	Number of incidents resolved without impact to the business

Table continues

Table 5.1 *continued*

Critical success factor	Key performance indicator
Maintain quality of IT services	Total numbers of incidents (as a control measure)
	Size of current incident backlog for each IT service
	Number and percentage of major incidents for each IT service
Maintain user satisfaction with IT services	Average user/customer survey score (total and by question category)
	Percentage of satisfaction surveys answered versus total number of satisfaction surveys sent
Increase visibility and communication of incidents to business and IT support staff	Average number of service desk calls or other contacts from business users for incidents already reported
	Number of business user complaints or issues about the content and quality of incident communications
Align incident management activities and priorities with those of the business	Percentage of incidents handled within agreed response time
	Average cost per incident

Critical success factor	Key performance indicator
Ensure that standardized methods and procedures are used for efficient and prompt response, analysis, documentation, ongoing management and reporting of incidents to maintain business confidence in IT capabilities	Number and percentage of incidents incorrectly assigned
	Number and percentage of incidents incorrectly categorized
	Number and percentage of incidents processed per service desk agent
	Number and percentage of incidents related to changes and releases

5.3.1.8 Challenges and risks (SO 4.2.9)

Challenges

- The ability to detect incidents as early as possible
- Convincing all staff that all incidents must be logged, encouraging the use of self-help facilities
- Availability of information about problems and known errors
- Integration with the configuration management system (CMS) and use of CI relationships and CI histories
- Integration with the SLM process, to correctly assess the impact and priority of incidents and assist in the use of escalation procedures.

Risks

- Being inundated with incidents that cannot be handled within acceptable timescales due to a lack of available or properly trained resources
- Unintended backlog of incidents created by inadequate support tools

- Lack of adequate or timely information sources because of poor tools or lack of integration
- Mismatches in objectives or actions because of poorly aligned or absent OLAs and/or UCs.

5.3.2   Problem management (SO 4.4) ☑

5.3.2.1   Purpose and objectives (SO 4.4.1) ✓

The purpose of problem management is to manage problems through their lifecycle from first identification through investigation, documentation and eventual resolution and closure. Problem management seeks to minimize the adverse impact of incidents and problems on the business caused by underlying errors within the IT Infrastructure, and to proactively prevent recurrence of incidents related to these errors.

The objectives of the problem management process are to:

- Prevent problems and resulting incidents from happening
- Eliminate recurring incidents
- Minimize the impact of incidents that cannot be prevented.

5.3.2.2   Scope (SO 4.4.2) ✓

Problem management includes the activities required to diagnose the root cause of incidents and to determine the cause and resolution of the underlying problems. It is also responsible for ensuring resolutions are implemented through the appropriate procedures, especially change management and release and deployment management.

Problem management maintains information about problems, workarounds and resolutions, enabling reductions in the number and impact of incidents over time, requiring a strong interface with knowledge management, and tools such as the known error database (KEDB).

Incident and problem management are separate processes but they typically use the same tools and similar categorization, impact and priority coding systems ensuring effective communication when dealing with related incidents and problems.

A close relationship exists between proactive problem management activities and CSI lifecycle activities that directly support identifying and implementing service improvements. Proactive problem management supports those activities through trending analysis and the targeting of preventive action. Identified problems from these activities become input to the continual service improvement (CSI) register.

5.3.2.3 Value to business (SO 4.4.3) ✗

The value of problem management includes:

- Higher availability of IT services by reducing the number and duration of incidents
- Higher productivity of IT staff by reducing unplanned activity caused by incidents and resolving incidents more quickly through the use of recorded known errors and workarounds
- Reduction in the cost of fire-fighting effort or resolving repeat incidents.

5.3.2.4   Principles and basic concepts (SO 4.4.4)

Definition: problem ✓

A problem is the cause of one or more incidents. The cause is not usually known at the time a problem record is created, and the problem management process is responsible for further investigation.

Definition: known error ✓

A known error is a problem that has a documented root cause and a workaround. Known errors are created and managed throughout their lifecycle by problem management. Known errors may also be identified by development or suppliers.

Definition: workaround ✓

A workaround is a way of reducing or eliminating the impact of an incident or problem for which a full resolution is not yet available – for example, by restarting a failed configuration item. Workarounds for problems are documented in known error records. Workarounds for incidents that do not have associated problem records are documented in the incident record.

Definition: known error database (KEDB) ✓

A database containing all known error records. This database is created by problem management and used by incident and problem management. The known error database may be part of the configuration management system, or may be stored elsewhere in the service knowledge management system.

Reactive and proactive problem management activities ✔

Both reactive and proactive problem management activities raise problems, manage them through the problem management process, find the underlying causes of the incidents and prevent future recurrences of those incidents. The difference is how the problem management process is triggered:

- **Reactive problem management** Triggered in reaction to an incident that has taken place, complementing incident management activities by focusing on the underlying cause of an incident to prevent its recurrence and identifying workarounds when necessary
- **Proactive problem management** Triggered by activities seeking to improve services, such as trend analysis activities, complementing CSI activities by helping to identify workarounds and improvement actions that can improve the quality of a service.

Problem models ✔

Many problems will be unique and require handling in an individual way. However some incidents may recur because of dormant or underlying problems (for example, where the cost of a permanent resolution will be high and a decision has been taken not to go ahead with an expensive solution but to 'live with' the problem).

As well as creating a known error record in the KEDB to ensure quicker diagnosis, a problem model can be created for handling such problems in the future.

Incidents versus problems ✔

An incident is an unplanned interruption to an IT service or reduction in the quality of an IT service. A problem presents a different view of an incident by understanding its underlying cause. Incidents do not 'become' problems. While incident management activities are focused on restoring services to normal state operations, problem management activities are focused on finding ways to prevent incidents from happening. It is quite common to have incidents that are also problems.

The rules for invoking problem management during an incident can vary at the discretion of individual organizations. Situations where it may be desired to invoke problem management during an incident include:

- Incident management cannot match an incident to existing problems and known errors
- Trend analysis of logged incidents reveals an underlying problem might exist
- A major incident has occurred where problem management needs to identify the root cause
- An incident is resolved but no definitive cause has been identified and it is likely to recur
- Analysis of an incident reveals that an underlying problem exists, or is likely to exist.

Problem management techniques ✗

There are many problem analysis, diagnosis and solving techniques available, including:

- Chronological analysis
- Pain value analysis
- Kepner-Tregoe
- Brainstorming
- 5-Whys
- Fault isolation
- Affinity mapping
- Hypothesis testing
- Technical observation post

- Ishikawa diagrams
- Pareto analysis.

5.3.2.5   Process activities, methods and techniques (SO 4.4.5) ✓

The key activities for problem management are:

- **Problem detection** By the service desk, technical support, event management, notification by a supplier, or from incident trend analysis.
- **Problem logging** All details must be recorded, including links to related incidents.
- **Problem categorization** Usually uses the same categorization codes as incidents.
- **Problem prioritization** Differs from incident prioritization in that this is based on frequency and impact of linked incidents, plus severity of the incident (impact on the infrastructure, cost to fix, time to fix).
- **Problem investigation and diagnosis** Determine root cause using techniques such as chronological analysis, pain value analysis, Kepner-Tregoe, brainstorming, Ishikawa diagram and Pareto analysis.
- **Workarounds** A workaround to the related incidents can reduce the impact of the problem until full resolution is achieved.
- **Raising a known error record** For use by the service desk to identify the symptoms and restore service quickly, using the workaround if one exists. Create when diagnosis is complete, but can raise earlier if useful.
- **Problem resolution** Usually requires a change request. If the resolution is not cost-effective, then the problem may be left open and the workaround should continue to be used.

- **Problem closure** After the change has been successfully reviewed – review related incident records, update known error records, check problem data and formally close.
- **Major problem review** A review of every major problem should be conducted to learn lessons for the future. Major problem is defined by the priority system.

5.3.2.6   Triggers ✗, inputs ✗, outputs ✗ and interfaces ✔ (SO 4.4.6)

Triggers

- Reactive problem management
- One or more incidents via service desk staff
- Other problem records, and corresponding known error records, e.g. during testing
- Supplier's notification of potential faults or known deficiencies
- Proactive problem management
- Identification of patterns and trends of incidents
- Reviews of other sources, e.g. operation or event logs, operation communications.

Inputs

- Incident records
- Incident reports for proactive problem trending
- Information about CIs and their status
- Communication about RFCs and releases
- Communication of events
- Operational and service level objectives
- Customer feedback
- Agreed criteria for prioritizing and escalating problems
- Output from risk management and risk assessment activities.

Outputs
- Resolved problems and resolution actions
- Updated problem management records
- RFCs
- Workarounds for incidents
- Known error records
- Problem management reports
- Output and improvement recommendations from major problem reviews.

Interfaces

Problem management provides a wealth of information and reports on the volumes and types of information to all other areas and processes, including:

- **Financial management for IT services** Assists in assessing the impact of proposed resolutions or workarounds, as well as pain value analysis, with problem management providing management information about the cost of resolving and preventing problems, which is used as input into the budgeting and accounting systems and total cost of ownership calculations.
- **Availability management** Uses proactive problem management to determine how to reduce downtime.
- **Capacity management** Assists with the investigation of some problems (e.g. performance issues), and with assessing proactive measures. Problem management provides management information relative to the quality of decision making during the capacity planning process.
- **ITSCM** Problem management acts as an entry point into ITSCM where a significant problem is not resolved before it starts to have a major impact on the business.
- **SLM** Problem management contributes to improvements in service levels by analysing incidents and problems affecting

the level of service, and its management information is used as the basis of SLA reviews. SLM also provides parameters within which problem management works, such as impact information and the effect on services of proposed resolutions and proactive measures.

- **Change management** Involves problem management in rectifying the situation caused by failed changes and problem management also ensures that all resolutions or workarounds that require a change to a CI are submitted through change management.

- **SACM** Provides the CMS which assists problem management to identify faulty CIs and also to determine the impact of problems and resolutions.

- **Release and deployment management** Is responsible for deploying problem fixes out into the live environment. It also assists in ensuring that the associated known errors are transferred from development into the live KEDB. Problem management also helps to resolve problems caused by faults during the release process.

- **Knowledge management** Provides the SKMS, which can be used to form the basis for the KEDB and record or integrate with the problem records.

- **Seven-step improvement process** Incidents and problems provide a basis for identifying opportunities for service improvement and adding them to the CSI register. Proactive problem management activities may also identify underlying problems and service issues that if addressed, can contribute to increases in service quality and end user/customer satisfaction.

5.3.2.7   Critical success factors and key performance indicators (SO 4.4.8) ✗

Table 5.2 includes some sample CSFs for problem management, followed by a small number of typical KPIs that support each CSF. Achievement against KPIs should be monitored and used to identify opportunities for improvement, which should be logged in the CSI register for evaluation and possible implementation.

Table 5.2 Examples of critical success factors and key performance indicators for problem management

Critical success factor	Key performance indicator
Minimize the impact to the business of incidents that cannot be prevented	The number of known errors added to the KEDB
	The percentage accuracy of the KEDB (from audits of the database)
	Percentage of incidents closed by the service desk without reference to other levels of support (often referred to as 'first point of contact')
	Average incident resolution time for those incidents linked to problem records

Table continues

Table 5.2 *continued*

Critical success factor	Key performance indicator
Maintain quality of IT services through elimination of recurring incidents	Total numbers of problems (as a control measure)
	Size of current problem backlog for each IT service
	Number of repeat incidents for each IT service
Provide overall quality and professionalism of problem handling activities to maintain business confidence in IT capabilities	The number of major problems (opened and closed and backlog)
	The percentage of major problem reviews completed successfully and on time
	The backlog of outstanding problems and the trend (static, reducing or increasing)
	Percentage of problems resolved within SLA targets
	Average cost per problem

5.3.2.8   Challenges and risks (SO 4.4.9) ✗

Challenges

- A major dependency for problem management is the establishment of an effective incident management process and tools
- The skills and capabilities for problem resolution staff to identify the true root cause of incidents

- The ability to relate incidents to problems can be a challenge if the tools used to record incidents are different from those of problems
- The ability to integrate problem management activities with the CMS to determine relationships between CIs and to refer to the history of CIs when performing problem support activities
- Ensuring that problem management is able to use all knowledge and SACM resources available to investigate and resolve problems
- Ensuring that ongoing training of technical staff in both technical aspects of their job as well as the business implications of the services they support and the processes they use is in place.

Risks

- Being inundated with problems that cannot be handled within acceptable timescales due to a lack of available or properly trained resources
- Problems being bogged down and not progressed as intended because of inadequate support tools for investigation
- Lack of adequate and/or timely information sources because of inadequate tools or lack of integration
- Problem support staff that may not be properly trained to investigate problems, find their underlying causes or identify appropriate actions to remove errors
- Mismatches in objectives or actions because of poorly aligned or non-existent OLAs and/or UCs.

5.3.3   Event management (SO 4.1) ✔

5.3.3.1   Purpose and objectives (SO 4.1.1) ✔

The purpose of event management is to manage events throughout their lifecycle. This lifecycle of activities to detect events, make sense of them and determine the appropriate control action is coordinated by the event management process.

Event management is therefore the basis for operational monitoring and control. If events are programmed to communicate operational information as well as warnings and exceptions, they can be used as a basis for automating many routine operations management activities.

The objectives of the event management process are to:

- Detect all changes of state that have significance for the management of a CI or IT service
- Determine the appropriate action for events and ensure communication to the appropriate functions
- Provide the trigger for the execution of many processes and operations management activities
- Provide comparison of actual operating performance against design standards and SLAs
- Provide a basis for service assurance and reporting; and service improvement.

5.3.3.2   Scope (SO 4.1.2) ✔

Event management can be applied to any aspect of service management that needs to be controlled and which can be automated. This includes:

- Monitoring and control of the status of CIs
- Environmental conditions

- Software licence monitoring to ensure optimum/legal licence utilization and allocation
- Security
- Normal activity.

5.3.3.3   Value to business (SO 4.1.3) ✗

Event management's value to the business is generally indirect; however, event management provides:

- Mechanisms for early detection of incidents and possible automated assignment to the appropriate group for action
- Automated monitoring by exception of activities, reducing downtime
- Integration with and improvement in the performance of other service management processes
- A basis for automated operations leading to increased efficiency
- A direct improvement in service delivery and customer satisfaction.

5.3.3.4   Principles and basic concepts (SO 4.1.4) ✗

Definition: event ✔

A change of state that has significance for the management of an IT service or other configuration item. The term is also used to mean an alert or notification created by any IT service, configuration item or monitoring tool. Events typically require IT operations personnel to take actions, and often lead to incidents being logged.

Types of events include:

- **Informational** For example, notification that a scheduled task has completed or a user has logged in

- **Warning** Typically generated when a threshold has been reached, enabling someone to react before things go wrong
- **Exception** A service or device is operating abnormally and action is required.

Definition: alert ✔

An alert is a notification that a threshold has been reached, something has changed, or a failure has occurred. Alerts are often created and managed by system management tools and are managed by the event management process.

5.3.3.5   Process activities, methods and techniques (SO 4.1.5) ✗

The key activities for event management are:

- **Event occurs** This event may not even be detected
- **Event notification** Either the CI generates a notification or a management tool detects a status change by polling
- **Event detection** By an agent running on the same system or a management tool
- **Event logged** The event should be recorded together with any actions taken
- **First level event correlation and filtering** To eliminate duplicates and unwanted events that cannot be disabled
- **Significance** Events are categorized as informational, warning or exception
- **Second level event correlation and filtering** Is normally performed by a 'correlation engine', usually part of a management tool that compares the event with a set of criteria and rules in a prescribed order. These are often referred to as business rules

- **Response selection** All events are logged; other responses might include automated recovery, alert and human intervention, logging an incident problem or change
- **Review actions** To check that significant events have been handled correctly
- **Close event**.

5.3.3.6   Triggers, inputs, outputs and interfaces (SO 4.1.6) ✗

Triggers

- Exceptions to any level of CI performance defined in the design specifications, OLAs or standard operating procedures (SOPs)
- Exceptions to an automated procedure or process
- An exception within a business process monitored by event management
- Completion of an automated task or job
- A status change in a server or database CI
- Access of an application or database by a user or automated procedure or job
- A predefined threshold is reached, e.g. by a device, database or application.

Inputs

- Operational and service level requirements (SLRs) associated with events
- Alarms, alerts and thresholds for recognizing events
- Event correlation tables, rules, event codes and automated response solutions
- Roles and responsibilities for recognizing and communicating events
- Operational procedures for recognizing, logging, escalating and communicating events.

Outputs
- Events communications and escalations
- Event logs
- Events that indicate an incident has occurred
- Events that indicate the potential breach of an SLA or OLA objective
- Events and alerts that indicate completion status of deployment, operational or other support activities
- Populated service knowledge management system (SKMS) with event information and history.

Interfaces
- **SLM** Ensures that any event with potential impact on SLAs is detected early and any failures are rectified as soon as possible.
- **ISM** Allows potentially significant business security events to be detected and acted upon.
- **Capacity and availability** Define significant events, thresholds and responses for event management to monitor, detect and respond to when they occur. Also event management should produce reports on patterns of events and potential areas of improvement.
- **SACM** Uses events to determine the current status of CIs in the infrastructure.
- **Knowledge management** Processes events for inclusion in knowledge management systems. For example, patterns of performance can be correlated with business activity and used as input into future design and strategy decisions.
- **Change management** Interfaces with event management to identify conditions that may require a response or action.
- **Incident and problem management** Require information on events that may require a response or action to resolve incidents and problems.
- **Access management** Events can be used to detect unauthorized access attempts and security breaches.

5.3.3.7 Critical success factors and key performance indicators (SO 4.1.8) ✗

Table 5.3 includes some sample CSFs for event management, followed by a small number of typical KPIs that support each CSF. Achievement against KPIs should be monitored and used to identify opportunities for improvement, which should be logged in the CSI register for evaluation and possible implementation.

Table 5.3 Examples of critical success factors and key performance indicators for event management

Critical success factor	Key performance indicator
Detecting changes of state that have significance for management of CIs and IT services	Number and ratio of events compared with the number of incidents
	Number and percentage of each type of event per platform or application versus total number of platforms and applications underpinning live IT services
Ensuring all events are communicated to the appropriate functions	Number and percentage of events that required human intervention and whether this was performed
	Number of incidents that occurred and percentage of these that were triggered without a corresponding event

Table continues

Table 5.3 *continued*

Critical success factor	Key performance indicator
Providing the trigger, or entry point, for the execution of many service operation processes and operations management activities	Number and percentage of events that required human intervention and whether this was performed
Provide the means to compare actual operating performance and behaviour against design standards and SLAs	Number and percentage of incidents that were resolved without impact to the business
	Number and percentage of events that resulted in incidents or changes
	Number and percentage of events caused by existing problems or known errors
	Number and percentage of events indicating performance issues
	Number and percentage of events indicating potential availability issues
Providing a basis for service assurance, reporting and service improvement	Number and percentage of repeated or duplicated events
	Number of events/alerts generated without actual degradation of service/ functionality

5.3.3.8   Challenges and risks (SO 4.1.9) ✕

Challenges

- An initial challenge may be to obtain funding for the necessary tools and effort needed to install and exploit the benefits of the tools
- One of the greatest challenges is setting the correct level of filtering
- Deploying the necessary monitoring agents across the entire IT infrastructure may be difficult and costly
- Automated monitoring activities can generate additional network traffic that might have negative impacts on planned capacity levels of the network
- Acquiring the necessary skills can be time-consuming and costly
- Deploying event management tools without setting up processes to deploy and operate them.

Risks

- Failure to obtain adequate funding
- Ensuring the correct level of filtering
- Failure to maintain momentum in deploying monitoring agents across the IT infrastructure.

5.3.4   Request fulfilment (SO 4.3) ✔

5.3.4.1   Purpose and objectives (SO 4.3.1) ✔

Request fulfilment is the process responsible for managing all service requests from the users through their lifecycle.

The objectives of the request fulfilment process are to:

- Maintain user and customer satisfaction through efficient and professional handling of service requests

- Provide a channel for users to request and receive standard services for which a predefined authorization and qualification process exists
- Provide information to users and customers about the availability of services and the procedure for obtaining them
- Source and deliver the components of requested standard services
- Assist with general information, complaints or comments.

5.3.4.2   Scope (SO 4.3.2) ✔

Some organizations handle service requests through their incident management process (and tools), with service requests being handled as a particular type of 'incident'. However there is a significant difference between an incident, usually an unplanned event, and a service request, which is something that should be planned. The process needed to fulfil a request varies depending upon exactly what is being requested, but can usually be broken down into a set of activities that have to be performed.

Therefore, in an organization where large numbers of service requests have to be handled, and where the actions to be taken to fulfil those requests are very varied or specialized, it may be appropriate to handle service requests as a completely separate work stream. Ultimately it is up to each organization to decide and document which service requests it handles through the request fulfilment process and which have to go through other processes.

5.3.4.3   Value to business (SO 4.3.3) ✘

The value of the request fulfilment process includes the ability:

- To provide effective access to standard services to business users improving productivity
- To effectively reduce the bureaucracy involved in gaining access to existing or new services

■ To increase the level of control over requested services through centralized fulfilment.

5.3.4.4 Principles and basic concepts (SO 4.3.4) ✔

Definition: service request ✔

A service request is a formal request from a user for something to be provided – for example, a request for information or advice; to reset a password; or to install a workstation for a new user. Service requests are managed by the request fulfilment process, usually in conjunction with the service desk. Service requests may be linked to a request for change as part of fulfilling the request.

Request models ✘

Service request models (which typically include one or more standard changes in order to complete fulfilment activities) should be defined, to ensure that frequently used service requests are handled consistently and meet agreed service levels.

Menu selection ✘

Request fulfilment offers great opportunities for self-help. Users should be offered a self-help menu from which they can select requests and provide details.

Financial approval ✘

The cost of providing the service should be established first and submitted to the user for approval within their management chain. In some cases there may be a need for additional compliance approval, or wider business approval.

5.3.4.5   Process activities, methods and techniques (SO 4.3.5) ✗

The key activities for request fulfilment are:

- **Receive request** Fulfilment of service request should not start until a formalized request has been received, normally by the service desk
- **Request logging and validation** All requests must be logged with the appropriate information and initially validated
- **Request categorization** Should involve allocating a suitable request categorization coding
- **Request prioritization** Involves the allocation of an appropriate priority to the request
- **Request authorization** No work should take place until the request has been properly authorized
- **Request review** Determines the function and need for the request is valid
- **Request model execution** Required activities and work flows are executed to fulfil the request
- **Request closure** Once completed the request should be closed
- **Rules for reopening requests** Predefined rules should exist for deciding when a closed service request can be reopened.

5.3.4.6   Triggers, inputs, outputs and interfaces (SO 4.3.6) ✗

Triggers

- Typically via a user calling the service desk or a user completing self-help web-based request form.

Inputs

- Work requests
- Authorization forms
- Service requests
- RFCs

- Requests from various sources such as phone calls, web interfaces or email
- Request for information.

Outputs

- Authorized/rejected service requests
- Request fulfilment status reports
- Fulfilled service requests
- Incidents (rerouted)
- RFCs/standard changes
- Asset/CI updates
- Updated request records
- Closed service requests
- Cancelled service requests.

Interfaces

- **Financial management for IT services** Interfaces may be needed if costs for fulfilling requests need to be reported and recovered.
- **Service catalogue management** Links with request fulfilment to ensure that requests are well known to users and linked with services in the catalogue that they support.
- **Release and deployment management** Some requests are for the deployment of new or upgraded components that can be automatically deployed.
- **SACM** Once deployed, the CMS has to be updated to reflect changes that may have been made as part of fulfilment activities.
- **Change management** Where a change is required to fulfil a request, it is logged as an RFC and progressed through change management.
- **Incident and problem management** Requests may come in via the service desk and may be initially handled through the incident management process.

■ **Access management** Ensures that those making requests are authorized to do so in accordance with the information security policy.

5.3.4.7 Critical success factors and key performance indicators (SO 4.3.8) ✗

Table 5.4 Examples of critical success factors and key performance indicators for request fulfilment

Critical success factor	Key performance indicator
Requests must be fulfilled in an efficient and timely manner that is aligned to agreed service level targets for each type of request	The mean elapsed time for handling each type of service request
	The number and percentage of service requests completed within agreed target times
	Breakdown of service requests at each stage
	Percentage of service requests closed by the service desk without reference to other levels of support
	Number and percentage of service requests resolved remotely or through automation, without the need for a visit
	Total numbers of requests (as a control measure)
	The average cost per type of service request

Critical success factor	Key performance indicator
Only authorized requests should be fulfilled	Percentage of service requests fulfilled that were appropriately authorized
	Number of incidents related to security threats from request fulfilment activities
User satisfaction must be maintained	Level of user satisfaction with the handling of service requests
	Total number of incidents related to request fulfilment activities
	The size of current backlog of outstanding service requests

Table 5.4 includes some sample CSFs for request fulfilment, followed by a small number of typical KPIs that support each CSF. Achievement against KPIs should be monitored and used to identify opportunities for improvement, which should be logged in the CSI register for evaluation and possible implementation.

5.3.4.8   Challenges and risks (SO 4.3.9) ✗

Challenges
- Clearly defining the type of requests to be handled by request fulfilment process
- Establishing self-help front-end capabilities that allow the users to interface successfully with the request fulfilment process
- Service level targets may be difficult to agree and establish
- The costs for fulfilling requests must also be agreed
- Agreements need to be in place for which services are standardized and who is authorized to request them

■ Information about what requests are available needs to be easily accessible
■ Requests need to follow a predefined standard fulfilment procedure
■ Request fulfilment has a very high impact on user satisfaction.

Risks

■ Poorly defined scope, where people are unclear about what the process is expected to handle
■ Poorly designed or implemented user interfaces so that users have difficulty raising requests
■ Badly designed or operated back-end fulfilment processes that are incapable of dealing with the volume or nature of the requests
■ Inadequate monitoring capabilities so that accurate metrics cannot be gathered.

5.3.5   Access management (SO 4.5) ✔

5.3.5.1   Purpose and objectives (SO 4.5.1) ✔

The purpose of access management is to provide the right for users to be able to use a service or group of services. It is therefore the execution of policies and actions defined in ISM.

The objectives of the access management process are to:

■ Manage access to services based on policies and actions defined by ISM
■ Efficiently respond to requests for granting access to services, changing access rights or restricting access, ensuring that the rights being provided or changed are properly granted
■ Oversee access to services and ensure rights being provided are not improperly used.

5.3.5.2   Scope (SO 4.5.2) ✔

Access management is effectively the execution of the policies in ISM, in that it enables the organization to manage the confidentiality, availability and integrity of the organization's data and intellectual property.

5.3.5.3   Value to business (SO 4.5.3) ✘

The value of access management includes:

■ Ensuring that controlled access to services allows the organization to maintain effective confidentiality of its information
■ Ensuring that employees have the right level of access to execute their jobs effectively
■ Reducing errors made in data entry or in the use of a critical service by an unskilled user
■ Providing capabilities to audit use of services and to trace the abuse of services
■ Providing capabilities to revoke access rights when needed on a timely basis
■ Providing and demonstrating compliance with regulatory requirements.

5.3.5.4   Principles and basic concepts (SO 4.5.4) ✘

Access management is the process that enables users to use the services that are documented in the service catalogue. It comprises the following basic concepts:

■ **Access** The service functionality or data that a user is entitled to use
■ **Identity** Information that distinguishes a user; each identity is unique
■ **Rights** The settings that enable a user to access a service

- **Services or service groups** Access is usually granted to groups of services, rather than to individual services
- **Directory services** A tool that is used to manage access and rights.

5.3.5.5   Process activities, methods and techniques (SO 4.5.5) ✗

The key activities in access management are:

- **Requesting access** This may come from a human resources system, an RFC, a service request or by executing a pre-authorized script or option from a staging server. The rules for requesting access are normally documented in the service catalogue.
- **Verification** Ensures that the user requesting access is who they say they are, and that they have a legitimate requirement. Usually requires independent verification.
- **Providing rights** Access management does not decide who has access; it executes policies and regulations defined during service strategy and design. It also manages requests for exceptions. Access management often sends requests to supporting teams to actually make the changes; where possible the granting of rights should be automated.
- **Monitoring identity status** Management of role changes due to job changes, promotions, transfers, resignation, death, retirement etc. The typical user lifecycle needs to be documented with tools to support the management of these changes.
- **Logging and tracking access** Access monitoring and control needs to be included in all service operation functions. Exceptions are handled by incident management, ideally using incident models. A record of access may be needed for use in forensic investigations; this is normally provided by operations management staff, but is part of the access management process.

■ **Removing or restricting rights** Access management is responsible for reducing and removing access rights, as well as providing them. Rights may need to be removed after death, resignation, dismissal or transfer to a different area; rights may be restricted if the user is under investigation (but still needs some services), when the user has changed roles and needs different access, or when the user is away on a temporary basis.

5.3.5.6   Triggers, inputs, outputs and interfaces (SO 4.5.6)

Triggers

■ An RFC
■ A service request
■ A request from human resources
■ A request from a manager.

Inputs

■ Information security policies
■ Operational and SLRs for granting access to services, performing access management administrative activities and responding to access management related events
■ Authorized RFCs to access rights
■ Authorized requests to grant or terminate access rights.

Outputs

■ Provision of access to IT services in accordance with information security policies
■ Access management records and history of access granted to services
■ Access management records and history where access was denied and the reasons for denial
■ Timely communications concerning inappropriate access or abuse of services.

Interfaces

- **Demand management** This process helps to identify the necessary resource levels to handle expected volumes of requests for access.
- **Strategy management for IT services** Some access management activities could be handled more efficiently within individual business organizations rather than in a centralized access management function.
- **ISM** Provides the security and data protection policies and tools needed to execute access management. Interfaces should also be in place with human resource processes to verify the user's identity as well, to ensure they are entitled to the services being requested.
- **Service catalogue management** Provides methods and means by which users can access different IT services, service descriptions and views that they are authorized for.
- **ITSCM** To manage access to services in the event of a major business disruption or where services have been provided from alternative locations.
- **SLM** Maintains the agreements for access to each service, including the criteria for who is entitled to access each service, what the cost of that access is, if appropriate, and what level of access can be granted to different types of user.
- **Change management** Controls the actual requests for access because access to a service is a change, although it is usually processed as a standard change or service request.
- **SACM** This process provides information on CIs to determine current access details.
- **Request fulfilment** This process provides methods and means by which users can request access to the standard services that are available to them.

5.3.5.7 Critical success factors and key performance indicators (SO 4.5.8) ✗

Table 5.5 Examples of critical success factors and key performance indicators for access management

Critical success factor	Key performance indicator
Ensuring that the confidentiality, integrity and availability of services are protected in accordance with the information security policy	Percentage of incidents that involved inappropriate security access or attempts at access to services
	Number of audit findings that discovered incorrect access settings for users that have changed roles or left the company
	Number of incidents requiring a reset of access rights
	Number of incidents caused by incorrect access settings
Provide appropriate access to services on a timely basis that meets business needs	Percentage of requests for access (service request, RFC etc.) that were provided within established SLAs and OLAs
Provide timely communications about improper access or abuse of services on a timely basis	Average duration of access-related incidents

Table 5.5 includes some sample CSFs for access management, followed by a small number of typical KPIs that support each CSF. Achievement against KPIs should be monitored and used to identify opportunities for improvement, which should be logged in the CSI register for evaluation and possible implementation.

5.3.5.8 Challenges and risks (SO 4.5.9)

Challenges

- Monitoring and reporting on access activity and incidents and problems related to access
- Verifying the identity of a user (that the person is who they say they are) and that the user qualifies for access to a specific service
- Verifying the identity of the approving person or body
- Linking multiple access rights to an individual user
- Determining the status of users at any time
- Managing changes to a user's access requirements
- Restricting access rights to unauthorized users
- Building and maintaining a database of all users and the rights that they have been granted.

Risks

- Lack of appropriate supporting technologies to manage and control access to services
- Controlling access from 'back door' sources such as application interfaces and changes to firewall rules for special needs
- Managing and controlling access to services by external third-party suppliers
- Lack of management support for access management activities and controls
- Ensuring that necessary levels of access to services and management controls are provided in a way that does not unnecessarily hinder the ability of users to conduct business.

5.4   ORGANIZING FOR SERVICE OPERATION (SO 6)

5.4.1   Service desk function (SO 6.3) ☑

The service desk is a vitally important part of an organization's IT department and is the single point of contact for IT users on a day-by-day basis. The service desk is key to the implementation of the request fulfilment and incident management processes.

A good service desk is often able to compensate for deficiencies elsewhere in the IT organization, but an ineffective service desk can give a poor impression of an otherwise very good IT organization. It is very important that the correct calibre of staff is used on the service desk and that IT managers make it an attractive place to work to improve staff retention.

5.4.1.1   Justification and role of the service desk (SO 6.3.1) ✓

The benefits of a good service desk include:

- Improved customer service, perception and satisfaction
- Single point of contact, communication and information
- Better quality and faster turnaround of customer or user requests
- Improved usage of IT support resources and increased productivity of users
- More meaningful management information for decision support.

5.4.1.2   Service desk objectives (SO 6.3.2) ✓

The service desk provides a single central point of contact for all users of IT. The service desk usually logs and manages all incidents, service requests and access requests and provides an interface for all other service operation processes and activities.

The primary aim of the service desk is to restore normal service as quickly as possible. This may involve fixing a technical fault, fulfilling a service request, or answering a query – anything that is needed to allow the users to return to normal working.

The specific responsibilities include:

- Logging all incidents and requests, categorizing and prioritizing them
- First-line investigation and diagnosis
- Managing the lifecycle of incidents and requests, escalating as appropriate and closing them when the user is satisfied
- Communicating with users, keeping them informed of incident progress
- Conducting customer/user satisfaction callbacks/surveys
- Updating the CMS under the direction and approval of configuration management if so agreed.

5.4.1.3   Service desk organizational structure (SO 6.3.3) ✓

There are many ways of structuring and locating service desks – the correct solution varies for different organizations. The primary options are detailed below and a combination of these may be needed in order to fully meet the business needs:

- **Local service desk** Co-located within or physically close to the user community it serves. This often aids communication, gives a clearly visible presence, and can support local language and cultural differences, but can often be inefficient and expensive to resource as the volume and arrival rate of calls may not justify the minimum staffing levels required.
- **Centralized service desk** The number of service desks can be reduced by merging them into a single location or a smaller number of locations. This can be more efficient and cost-effective, allowing fewer staff to deal with a higher volume

of calls. It might still be necessary to maintain some 'local presence', but such staff can be controlled and deployed from the central desk.

- **Virtual service desk** Through the use of technology, particularly the Internet, and corporate support tools, it is possible to give the impression of a single, centralized service desk when in fact the personnel may be in any number or types of locations. This gives the option of 'home working', offshoring or outsourcing – or any combination necessary to meet user demand.

- **Follow the sun** Some global or international organizations may combine two or more of their geographically dispersed service desks to provide a 24-hour follow-the-sun service. This can give 24-hour coverage at relatively low cost, as no desk has to work more than a single shift. However, common processes, tools, a shared database of information, and robust handover procedures are needed for this to be successful.

- **Specialized service desk groups** Some organizations find it beneficial to create specialist groups within the overall service desk structure, so that incidents relating to a particular IT service can be routed directly to the specialist group, allowing faster resolution of these incidents, through greater familiarity and specialist training.

5.4.2 Technical management function (SO 6.4) ✔

5.4.2.1 Technical management role (SO 6.4.1) ✔

Technical management plays a dual role:

- It is the custodian of technical knowledge and expertise related to managing the IT infrastructure. In this role, technical management ensures that the knowledge required to design, test, manage and improve IT services is identified, developed and refined

■   It provides the actual resources to support the service
lifecycle. In this role technical management ensures that
resources are effectively trained and deployed to design,
build, transition, operate and improve the technology
required to deliver and support IT services.

Part of the role is also to ensure a balance between the skill level,
utilization and cost of these resources. An additional but very
important role played by technical management is to provide
guidance to IT operations about how best to carry out the
ongoing operational management of technology.

5.4.2.2   Technical management objectives (SO 6.4.2) ✔

The objectives of technical management are to help plan,
implement and maintain a stable technical infrastructure to
support the organization's business processes through:

■   Well designed and highly resilient, cost-effective technical
topology
■   The use of adequate technical skills to maintain the technical
infrastructure in optimum condition
■   Swift use of technical skills to speedily diagnose and resolve
any technical failures that do occur.

5.4.2.3   Generic technical management activities (SO 6.4.3) ✘

Technical management is involved in two types of activity:

■   Activities that are generic to the technical management
function as a whole, in support of managing and operating
the IT services and infrastructure. These activities are
summarized below.
■   A set of discrete activities and processes performed by all
three functions of technical, application and IT operations
management, depending on the technology being managed,
e.g. network and storage management.

The generic technical management activities required to manage and operate IT service and infrastructure include:

- Identifying knowledge and expertise requirements to manage and operate IT infrastructure and to deliver IT services
- Identifying skills requirements for technical staff, initiating training programmes, recruiting or contracting resources
- Design and delivery of user training
- Involvement in the design and build of new services and operational practices
- Contributing to service design, service transition or CSI projects
- Assistance with service management processes, helping to define standards and tools, and undertaking activities such as the evaluation of change requests
- Assistance with the management of suppliers, contracts and vendors.

5.4.3 IT operations management function (SO 6.5) ✔

5.4.3.1 IT operations management role (SO 6.5.1) ✔

The role of IT operations management is to execute the ongoing activities and procedures required to manage and maintain the IT infrastructure so as to deliver and support IT services at the agreed levels.

As with many ITSM processes and functions, IT operations management plays a dual role and must achieve the right balance between the two roles:

- The stability of the IT infrastructure and consistency of IT services is a primary concern of IT operations
- IT operations must also continually adapt to new and changing business requirements and demand.

IT operations management includes two functions:

- **IT operations control** Staffed by shifts of operators who carry out routine operational tasks. They provide centralized monitoring and control, usually from an operations bridge or network operations centre. Specific activities include:
  - Console management – defining and operating a central observation and monitoring capability
  - Job scheduling – the management of routine batch jobs or scripts
  - Backup and restore – on behalf of all technical and application management teams and departments and often on behalf of users
  - Print and output management
  - Maintenance activities – on behalf of technical or application management teams or departments.
- **Facilities management** Responsible for the management of data centres, computer rooms and recovery sites together with their power and cooling requirements. Facilities management also coordinates large-scale projects, such as data centre consolidation or server consolidation.

5.4.3.2 IT operations management objectives (SO 6.5.2) ✔

The objectives of IT operations management include:

- Achieving stability of the organization's day-to-day processes and activities
- Continual improvements to improve service at reduced costs, while maintaining stability
- Rapid diagnosis and resolution of any IT operational failures that occur.

5.4.4   Application management function (SO 6.6) ✔

5.4.4.1   Application management role (SO 6.6.1) ✔

Application management is responsible for managing applications throughout their lifecycle. This differs from application development as application management covers the entire ongoing lifecycle of an application, including requirements, design, build, deploy, operate and optimize. The application management function is performed by any department, group or team involved in managing and supporting operational applications. Application management also plays an important role in the design, testing and improvement of applications that form part of IT services.

Application management activities are performed in all applications, whether purchased or developed in-house. One of the key decisions that they contribute to is the decision of whether to buy an application or build it. Once that decision is made, application management has several roles:

- It is the custodian of technical knowledge and expertise related to managing applications. In this role application management, working together with technical management, ensures that the knowledge required to design, test, manage and improve IT services is identified, developed and refined

- It provides the actual resources to support the service lifecycle. In this role, application management ensures that resources are effectively trained and deployed to design, build, transition, operate and improve the technology required to deliver and support IT services.

By performing these roles, application management is able to ensure that the organization has access to the right type and level of human resources to manage applications and thus to meet business objectives. Application management also performs other specific roles:

■ Providing guidance to IT operations about how best to carry out the ongoing operational management of applications

■ Integration of the application management lifecycle into the service lifecycle.

5.4.4.2   Application management objectives (SO 6.6.2) ✔

The objectives of application management are:

■ To support the organization's business processes by helping identify functional and manageability requirements for application software

■ To assist in the design and deployment of applications and the ongoing support and improvement of those applications.

These objectives are achieved through:

■ Designing applications that are resilient and cost-effective

■ Ensuring that the required functionality is available to achieve the required business outcome

■ Organizing technical skills to maintain operational applications in optimum condition

■ Using technical skills to speedily diagnose and resolve technical failures that occur.

5.4.4.3   Application management lifecycle (SO 6.6.4) ✘

The lifecycle followed to develop and manage applications has been referred to by many names. ITIL is primarily interested in the overall management of applications as part of IT services, whether they are developed in-house or purchased from a third party. For this reason, the term application management lifecycle has been used, as it implies a more holistic view as shown in Figure 5.1.

Figure 5.1 Application management lifecycle

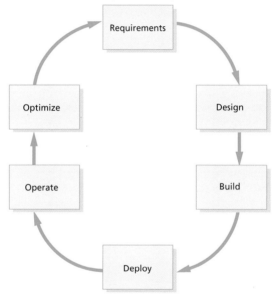

ITSM and applications development processes have to be aligned throughout this lifecycle as part of the overall strategy for delivering IT services in support of the business. Applications development and operations are part of the same overall lifecycle and both should be involved at all stages, although their level of involvement varies depending on the stage of the lifecycle:

- ■ **Requirements** Is where the functional, manageability and usability requirements of a new application are gathered and agreed
- ■ **Design** Is where the requirements are translated into specifications for the solution
- ■ **Build** Is where the application is assembled, tested and made ready for deployment
- ■ **Deploy** Is where the application is deployed to the operational environment
- ■ **Operate** Is where the application is operated as part of delivering a service needed by the business
- ■ **Optimize** Is where service levels are measured and compared with targets. Possible improvements are discussed and initiated as necessary.

5.4.4.4 Application development versus application management (SO 6.6.6.1) ✔

Often, application development and management teams and departments have acted as autonomous units. Each one manages its own environment in its own way and each has a separate interface to the business. This is illustrated in Table 5.6.

Recently these two areas have been working closer together, with growing pressure from the business to be more responsive. Application development will become more accountable for the successful operation of applications they design, while application management will move towards greater involvement in the development of applications. This does not change the fundamental role of each group, but it does require a more integrated approach between application development and application management functions.

Table 5.6 Application development versus application management

	Application development	Application management
Nature of activities	One-time set of activities to design and construct application solutions	Ongoing set of activities to oversee and manage applications throughout their entire lifecycle
Scope of activities	Performed mostly for applications developed in-house	Performed for all applications, whether purchased from third parties or developed in-house
Primary focus	Utility focus Building functionality for their customer What the application does is more important than how it is operated	Both utility and warranty focus What the functionality is as well as how to deliver it Manageability aspects of the application, i.e. how to ensure stability and performance of the application

Table continues

Table 5.6 *continued*

	Application development	Application management
Management mode	Most development work is done in projects where the focus is on delivering specific units of work to specification, on time and within budget This means that it is often difficult for developers to understand and build for ongoing operations, especially because they are not available for support of the application once they have moved on to the next project	Most work is done as part of repeatable, ongoing processes. A relatively small number of people work in projects This means that it is very difficult for operational staff to get involved in development projects, as that takes them away from their ongoing operational responsibilities
Measurement	Staff are typically rewarded for creativity and for completing one project so that they can move on to the next project	Staff are typically rewarded for consistency and for preventing unexpected events and unauthorized functionality (e.g. 'bells and whistles' added by developers)

	Application development	Application management
Cost	Development projects are relatively easy to quantify because the resources are known and it is easy to link their expenses to a specific application or IT service	Ongoing management costs are often mixed in with the costs of other IT services because resources are often shared across multiple IT services and applications
Lifecycles	Development staff focus on software development lifecycles, which highlight the dependencies for successful operation, but do not assign accountability for these	Staff involved in ongoing management typically only control one or two stages of these lifecycles – operation and improvement

5.5   TECHNOLOGY CONSIDERATIONS ✗

Each function and process requires technology to work effectively. This can be achieved more efficiently with an integrated set of service management technology for service operation. The same technology, with some possible additions, should also be used for the other stages of the service lifecycle to give consistency and to allow the service lifecycle to be properly managed.

5.5.1 Generic requirements

An integrated ITSM technology (or toolset, as some suppliers sell their technology as 'modules' whereas some organizations may choose to integrate products from alternative suppliers) is needed that includes the following core functionality.

- **Self-help** Some form of web front-end allowing web pages to be defined offering a menu-driven range of self-help and service requests – with a direct interface into the back-end process-handling software.
- **Workflow or process engine** Allows the definition and control of processes such as an incident lifecycle, request fulfilment, problem lifecycle, change model etc. and allows responsibilities, activities, timescales, escalations and alerting to be automatically managed.
- **Integrated CMS** Allows infrastructure assets, components and services to be held as CIs, together with relevant attributes, in a centralized location with relationships between each to be maintained.
- **Discovery/deployment/licensing technology** Can populate or verify the CMS data and assist in licence management, discovery or automated audit.
- **Remote control** Allow analysts to take control of the user's desktop (so as to allow them to conduct investigations or correct settings).
- **Diagnostic utilities** Help create and use diagnostic scripts and other diagnostic utilities to help with earlier diagnosis of incidents.
- **Reporting** Supporting good reporting capabilities, as well as allowing standard interfaces which can be used to input data to industry-standard reporting packages, dashboards on screen as well as printed.

■ **Dashboards** Allow 'see at a glance' visibility of overall IT service performance and availability levels.

5.5.2 Specific requirements

Specific technology requirements are also required in each of the following areas. Again these requirements are best provided by an integrated ITSM toolset:

■ Event management
■ Incident management
■ Request fulfilment
■ Problem management
■ Access management
■ Service desk.

6   Continual service improvement

ITIL Continual Service Improvement provides guidance on creating and maintaining value for customers through better strategy, design, transition and operation of services. It combines principles, practices and methods from quality management, change management and capability improvement.

ITIL Continual Service Improvement describes best practice for achieving incremental and large-scale improvements in service quality, operational efficiency and business continuity, and for ensuring that the service portfolio continues to be aligned to business needs. Guidance is provided for linking improvement efforts and outcomes with service strategy, design, transition and operation. A closed loop feedback system, based on the Plan-Do-Check-Act (PDCA) cycle, is established. Feedback from any stage of the service lifecycle can be used to identify improvement opportunities for any other stage of the lifecycle.

6.1   PURPOSE, OBJECTIVES, SCOPE AND VALUE OF CONTINUAL SERVICE IMPROVEMENT

6.1.1   Purpose and objectives (CSI 1.1.1) ✔

The purpose of the CSI stage of the lifecycle is to align IT services with changing business needs by identifying and implementing improvements to IT services that support business processes. These improvement activities support the lifecycle approach through service strategy, service design, service transition and service operation. CSI is always seeking ways to improve service effectiveness, process effectiveness and cost effectiveness.

The objectives of CSI are to:

■ Review, analyse, prioritize and make recommendations on improvement opportunities in each lifecycle stage: service strategy, service design, service transition, service operation and CSI itself

■ Review and analyse service level achievement

■ Identify and implement specific activities to improve IT service quality and improve the efficiency and effectiveness of the enabling processes

■ Improve cost effectiveness of delivering IT services without sacrificing customer satisfaction

■ Ensure applicable quality management methods are used to support continual improvement activities

■ Ensure that processes have clearly defined objectives and measurements that lead to actionable improvements

■ Understand what to measure, why it is being measured and what the successful outcome should be.

6.1.2 Scope (CSI 1.1.2) ✔

ITIL Continual Service Improvement provides guidance in four main areas:

■ The overall health of ITSM as a discipline

■ The continual alignment of the service portfolio with the current and future business needs

■ The maturity and capability of the organization, management, processes and people utilized by the services

■ Continual improvement of all aspects of the IT service and the service assets that support them.

6.1.3 Value to business (CSI 1.1.4) ✔

Adopting and implementing standard and consistent approaches for CSI:

- Leads to a gradual and continual improvement in service quality, where justified
- Ensures that IT services remain continuously aligned to business requirements
- Results in gradual improvements in cost effectiveness through a reduction in costs and/or the capability to handle more work at the same cost
- Uses monitoring and reporting to identify opportunities for improvement in all lifecycle stages and in all processes
- Identifies opportunities for improvements in organizational structures, resourcing capabilities, partners, technology, staff skills and training, and communications.

6.2 KEY PRINCIPLES

Service improvement must focus on increasing the efficiency, maximizing the effectiveness and optimizing the cost of services and the underlying IT service management (ITSM) processes. The only way to do this is to ensure that improvement opportunities are identified throughout the entire service lifecycle.

6.2.1 Continual service improvement approach (CSI 3.1) ✔

Figure 6.1 Continual service improvement approach

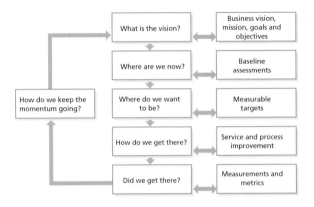

Figure 6.1 shows an overall approach to CSI and illustrates a continual cycle of improvement. This approach to improvement can be summarized as follows:

- **What is the vision?** Understand high-level business objectives and align business and IT strategies.
- **Where are we now?** Assess the current situation to obtain an accurate, unbiased snapshot of where the organization is now, including the business, organization, people, process and technology.
- **Where do we want to be?** Understand and agree on the priorities for improvement based on the vision. The full vision

may be years away but this step provides specific goals and a manageable timeframe.

- **How do we get there?** Detail the CSI plan to achieve higher quality service provision by implementing or improving ITSM processes.

- **Did we get there?** Verify that measurements and metrics are in place and that the milestones were achieved, process compliance is high, and business objectives and priorities were met.

- **How do we keep the momentum going?** Ensure the momentum for quality improvement is maintained by assuring that changes become embedded in the organization.

There is a common belief that CSI activities cannot improve a service that doesn't yet exist and that the service has to be operational to identify improvement opportunities. However, CSI can add value in designing a new service by bringing the knowledge and experience from improving existing services. CSI can proactively prevent the potential flaws in the new service. CSI activities can be executed within service strategy, service design, service transition and service operation.

6.2.2 Continual service improvement and organizational change (CSI 3.2) ✗

Improving service management often requires an organizational change programme, but many organizational change programmes fail to achieve the desired results. Successful ITSM requires understanding the way in which work is done and putting in place a programme of change within the IT organization. This type of change is, by its very nature, prone to difficulties. It involves people and the way they work. People generally do not like to change; the benefits must be explained to everyone to gain their support and to ensure that they break out of old working practices.

6.2.3   Ownership (CSI 3.3) ✗

The principle of ownership is fundamental to any improvement strategy. CSI is a best practice and one of the keys to successful implementation is to ensure that a specific manager, a CSI manager, is accountable for ensuring that best practice is adopted and sustained throughout the organization. The CSI manager is the chief advocate and owns all CSI issues. The CSI manager is accountable for the success of CSI in the organization.

While the CSI manager is responsible and accountable for CSI, the CSI manager is not accountable for improvements to specific services. Specific service improvements are the responsibility of the appropriate service owner working within the framework of CSI.

6.2.4   Continual service improvement register (CSI 3.4) ✔

Many initiatives or possibilities for improvement may be identified and it is recommended that a CSI register is kept to record all improvement opportunities. Each opportunity should be categorized into small, medium or large undertakings and also categorized into initiatives that can be achieved quickly, or in the medium term or longer term. Each improvement initiative should also show the benefits that will be achieved by its implementation. With this information a clear prioritized list can be produced. A common problem with prioritization is that once something has been identified as a low priority it often stays at that level and never gets addressed. An automatic raising of priority over time may be a useful addition to management of the register.

The CSI register contains important information for the overall service provider and should be held and regarded as part of the service knowledge management system (SKMS).

The CSI manager should have accountability and responsibility for the production and maintenance of the CSI register.

6.2.5   Continual service improvement and service level management (CSI 3.6) ✗

Adopting the service level management (SLM) process is a key principle of CSI. While in the past many IT organizations viewed SLM as merely a number of isolated agreements around system availability or service desk calls, this is no longer true. SLM is no longer optional. Business now demands that IT is driven by service requirements and outcomes. This service orientation of IT toward the business becomes the foundation for the trusted partnership that IT must endeavour to create.

A key step in the SLM process is to review service achievement, identify where improvements are required, and to feed them into CSI and the CSI register.

6.2.6   Continual service improvement and knowledge management (CSI 3.7) ✗

'Those who cannot remember the past are condemned to repeat it.'
George Santayana

Knowledge management is explained fully in *ITIL Service Transition* (see also section 4.3.7 in this publication) but it plays a key role in CSI. Within each service lifecycle stage, data should be captured to enable knowledge gain and an understanding of what is actually happening, thus enabling wisdom. All too often an organization captures the appropriate data but fails to process the data into information, synthesize the information into knowledge, and then combine that knowledge with others to bring wisdom. Wisdom leads to better decisions around improvement.

This applies both when looking at the IT services themselves and when drilling down into each individual IT process. Knowledge management is a mainstay of any improvement process.

6.2.7 The Deming Cycle/PDCA cycle (CSI 3.8) ✔

The Deming Cycle (Plan-Do-Check-Act or PDCA cycle) is widely used as the foundation for quality improvement activities across many types of organization.

PDCA forms a fundamental part of many quality standards including ISO/IEC 20000.

- **Plan** Clearly document the target state and the intended steps to get there
- **Do** Execute the plan
- **Check** Monitor and measure outcomes to determine actual achievements against the plan
- **Act** Identify gaps against expectations and opportunities for further improvement.

Following each pass through the cycle there is a phase of consolidation to ensure that improvements and benefits are not temporary.

The PDCA cycle is critical at two points in CSI: implementation of CSI, and for the application of CSI to services and service management processes. At implementation, all four stages of the PDCA cycle are used. With ongoing improvement, CSI draws on the check and act stages to monitor, measure, review and implement initiatives.

6.2.8 Service measurement (CSI 3.9) ✔

6.2.8.1 Why do we measure? (CSI 3.9.2) ✗

There are four reasons to monitor and measure:

- **To validate** previous decisions
- **To direct** activities in order to meet set targets; it is the most prevalent reason for monitoring and measuring
- **To justify** with factual evidence or proof that a course of action is required
- **To intervene,** including subsequent changes and corrective actions.

6.2.8.2 Baselines (CSI 3.9.1) ✔

An important starting point for any improvement activity is establishing a baseline. In the context of CSI, a baseline provides the current state of a configuration item (CI), process or any other data recorded at a specific point in time, and is used as a reference point for future comparisons. For example, an ITSM baseline can be used as a starting point to measure the effect of a service improvement plan (SIP); a performance baseline can be used to measure changes in performance over the lifetime of an IT service.

It is essential to collect baseline data at the outset, even if the integrity of the data is in question. It is better to have baseline data to question than to have no baseline data at all.[1]

---

1 Baselines can be used for other purposes. See section 4.3.3.4 regarding configuration baselines.

6.2.9   Metrics, KPIs and CSFs (CSI 5.5, 5.5.1) ✔

6.2.9.1   Metrics ✔

> **Definition: metric** ✔
>
> Something that is measured and reported to help manage a process, IT service or activity.

There are three types of metrics that an organization needs to collect to support CSI and other activities:

- **Technology metrics** These metrics are often associated with component and application-based metrics such as performance, availability etc.
- **Process metrics** These metrics are captured in the form of critical success factors (CSFs), KPIs and activity metrics for service management processes. They can help determine the overall health of a process and focus on quality, performance, value and compliance.
- **Service metrics** These metrics are a measure of the end-to-end service performance. Individual technology and process metrics are used when calculating the end-to-end service metrics.

In general, a metric is a scale of measurement defined in terms of a standard, i.e. a well-defined unit. Metrics are usually specialized by the subject area, in which case they are valid only within a certain domain and cannot be directly benchmarked or interpreted outside it. Generic metrics, however, can be aggregated across subject areas or business units of an enterprise.

Metrics are used in several business models including CMMI, COBIT and Six Sigma. These measurements or metrics can be used to track trends, productivity, resources and much more. Typically, the metrics tracked are KPIs as discussed below.

6.2.9.2   Critical success factor ✔

Definition: critical success factor (CSF) ✔

Something that must happen if an IT service, process, plan, project or other activity is to succeed. Key performance indicators are used to measure the achievement of each critical success factor. For example, a critical success factor of 'protect IT services when making changes' could be measured by key performance indicators such as 'percentage reduction of unsuccessful changes', 'percentage reduction in changes causing incidents' etc.

6.2.9.3   Key performance indicator ✔

Definition: key performance indicator (KPI) ✔

A metric that is used to help manage an IT service, process, plan, project or other activity. Key performance indicators are used to measure the achievement of critical success factors. Many metrics may be measured, but only the most important of these are defined as key performance indicators and used to actively manage and report on the process, IT service or activity. They should be selected to ensure that efficiency, effectiveness and cost effectiveness are all managed.

There are two basic kinds of KPI, qualitative and quantitative. Qualitative KPIs relate to the quality or character of something, whereas quantitative KPIs relate to size or quantity. Examples of each are provided later in this subsection.

An important aspect to consider is whether a KPI is fit for use. Example questions are:

- What does the performance indicator tell us about goal achievement? If we fail to meet the target set for a performance indicator, does that mean we fail to achieve some of our goals? And if we succeed in meeting certain targets, does this mean we will achieve our goals?
- How easy is it to interpret the performance indicator? Does it help us to decide on a course of action?
- To what extent is the performance indicator stable and accurate? Is it sensitive to external, uncontrollable influences?
- Which conditions impede measurement? Which conditions render the result meaningless?

It is recommended that in the early stages of a CSI initiative only two to three KPIs for each CSF are defined, monitored and reported on. As the maturity of a service and service management processes increase, additional KPIs can be added. Based on what is important to the business and IT management, KPIs may change over a period of time, plus as service management processes are implemented, this can often change the KPIs of other processes. As an example, increasing first-contact resolution is a common KPI for incident management. This is a good KPI to begin with, but when problem management is implemented, this should change. One of problem management's objectives is to reduce the number of recurring incidents. When these types of recurring incidents are reduced it will reduce the number of first-contact resolutions. In this case a reduction in first-contact resolution is a positive trend.

Examples of CSFs and KPIs are provided within each process subsection in this publication. It is recommended that no more than two to five KPIs are defined per CSF at any given time and that a service or process has no more than two to five CSFs associated with it at any given time.

6.2.9.4 From vision to measurements ✔

Figure 6.2 From vision to measurements

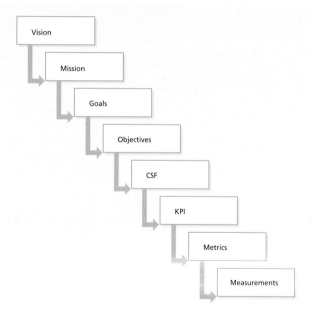

Figure 6.2 shows the full hierarchy from vision to measurements and the role that metrics, KPIs and CSFs fulfil in this hierarchy.

To help illustrate this relationship, here are two examples of how metrics, KPIs and measurements are used to support CSFs, and ultimately the vision.

Qualitative example

- CSF: Improving IT service quality
- KPI: 10% increase in customer satisfaction rating for handling incidents over the next six months.

Metrics required:

- Original customer satisfaction score for handling incidents
- Ending customer satisfaction score for handling incidents.

Measurements:

- Incident-handling survey score
- Number of survey scores.

Quantitative example

- CSF: Reducing IT costs
- KPI: 10% reduction in the costs of handling printer incidents.

Metrics required:

- Original cost of handling printer incidents
- Final cost of handling printer incidents
- Cost of the improvement effort.

Measurements:

- Time spent on the incident by first- and second-level operatives and their average salaries
- Time spent on problem management activities by second-level operatives and their average salary

- Time spent on training the first-level operative on the workaround.

6.2.10 Assessments, benchmarking and gap analysis (CSI 5.2, 5.3) ✗

6.2.10.1 Assessments ✗

An assessment is a technique for inspecting and analysing whether a standard or set of guidelines is being followed, that records are accurate, or that efficiency and effectiveness targets are being met. By conducting a formal assessment an organization is demonstrating a significant level of commitment to improvement. Identifying and dealing with any issues and gaps identified during an assessment makes a key contribution to the seven-step improvement process.

Section 6.2.8 introduced the concept of a baseline which provides the current state of a CI, process or any other data recorded at a specific point in time. Baselines can be used for comparison purposes and an assessment is a common technique for establishing such a baseline. Baselines used for comparison purposes are also known as benchmarks.

6.2.10.2 Benchmarking ✗

Benchmarking is the process of comparing a benchmark with related data sets such as a more recent baseline, industry data or best practice. The term is also used to mean creating a series of benchmarks over time, and comparing the results to measure progress or improvement.

Benchmarking is often used by organizations to evaluate various aspects of their processes against best practice, usually within their own sector. The results of assessments and benchmarking lead to the identification of gaps in terms of people, process and technology. A benchmark can highlight the benefits of improvement as well as the risks arising from not addressing gaps.

Benchmarking often reveals quick wins – opportunities for improvement that are relatively easy and inexpensive to implement while providing substantial benefits in process effectiveness, cost reduction or staff synergy.

6.2.10.3 Gap analysis ✗

A gap analysis is an activity that compares two sets of data and identifies any differences between them. Gap analysis builds on assessment and benchmarking and allows comparisons to be made between actual performance and expected performance, and can be performed at the strategic, tactical or operational level of an organization.

Gap analysis can be conducted from different perspectives such as:

- The organization, including organizational structure and capabilities of the people
- Business direction
- Business processes
- IT.

Gap analysis provides a foundation for how much effort in time, money and human resources is required to achieve a particular goal – for example, how to bring a service from one level of maturity to another.

6.2.11 Service reporting (CSI 5.7 ✗, CSI Figure 4.4 ✔)

Service reporting is a set of activities that produce and deliver reports of achievement and trends against service levels. The format, content and frequency of reports should be agreed with customers.

A significant amount of data is collated and monitored by IT in the daily delivery of quality service to the business; however, only a small subset is of real interest and importance to the business. Most data and its meaning are more suited to the internal management needs of IT.

The business likes to see a historical representation of past performance that relates to its own experience. However, it is more concerned with those historical events that continue to be a threat going forward, and how IT intends to militate against such threats. Data should also be provided that aligns to any contracted, chargeable elements of service delivery, which may or may not be technical depending on the business focus and the language used within contracts and SLAs.

It is not satisfactory simply to present reports that depict adherence (or otherwise) to SLAs, which in themselves are prone to statistical ambiguity. IT needs to build an actionable approach to reporting: this is what happened, this is what we did, this is how we will ensure it doesn't impact you again, and this is how we are working to improve the delivery of IT services generally.

Recipients should be provided with clear, unambiguous and relevant information in a language and style that they understand and like, and is available in the medium of their choice, i.e. 'the right content for the right audience'.

A reporting ethos that focuses on the future as strongly as it focuses on the past also provides the means for IT to promote what it does in a way that is directly aligned to the positive or negative experiences of the business.

Figure 6.3 is an example of an SLA monitoring chart (SLAM chart) that provides a visual representation of an organization's ability to meet defined targets over a period of months. Section 3.3.2.4 provides a description of an SLAM chart.

Figure 6.3 Service level achievement chart

Target / Period	January	February	March	April	May	June	July	August
A								
B								
C								
D								
E								
F								

Target met   Target breached   Target threatened

6.3   PROCESSES AND ACTIVITIES

6.3.1   The seven-step improvement process
(CSI 3.9.3.1, CSI 4.1) ✔

Figure 6.4 The seven-step improvement process

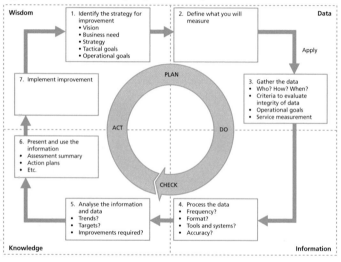

Figure 6.4 shows the seven-step improvement process and its interaction with the PDCA cycle (see section 6.2.7) and the CSI approach (see section 6.2.1). The figure also shows how each of these elements aligns with the Data-to-Information-to-Knowledge-to-Wisdom (DIKW) structure of knowledge management (see section 4.3.7.4).

6.3.1.1   Purpose and objectives (CSI 4.1.1) ✔

The purpose of the seven-step improvement process is to define and manage the steps needed to identify, define, gather, process, analyse, present and implement improvements.

The objectives of the seven-step improvement process are to:

■ Identify opportunities for improving services, processes, tools etc.
■ Reduce the cost of providing services and ensuring that IT services enable the required business outcomes to be achieved
■ Identify what needs to be measured, analysed and reported to establish improvement opportunities
■ Continually review service achievements to ensure they remain matched to business requirements; continually align and re-align service provision with outcome requirements
■ Understand what to measure, why it is being measured and carefully define the successful outcome.

Improvements in quality should not be implemented if there is a cost associated with the improvement and if this cost has not been justified. Every potential improvement opportunity should have a business case justification to show that the business will have an overall benefit.

6.3.1.2   Scope (CSI 4.1.2) ✔

The seven-step improvement process includes analysis of the performance and capabilities of services, processes throughout the lifecycle, partners and technology. It includes the continual alignment of the portfolio of IT services with the current and future business needs as well as the maturity of the enabling IT processes for each service. It also includes making best use of the technology that the organization has and looks to exploit new technology as it becomes available where there is a business case for doing so. Also within the scope are the organizational structure, the capabilities of the personnel, and asking whether people are working in appropriate functions and roles, and if they have the required skills.

6.3.1.3 Value to business (CSI 4.1.3) ✗

By monitoring and analysing the delivery of services, the seven-step improvement process ensures that current and future business outcome requirements can be met. The process enables continual assessment of the current situation against business needs and identifies opportunities to improve service provision for customers.

6.3.1.4 Principles and basic concepts (CSI 4.1.4) ✗

Many service providers operate in a competitive environment and they need to continually assess their services against market expectations to ensure they remain competitive. Also, new delivery mechanisms (e.g. cloud computing) can introduce service efficiencies and need to be reviewed. The following activities should be regularly performed:

- Services must be checked against competitive service offerings to ensure they continue to add true business value to the client, and the service provider remains competitive
- Services must be reviewed in the light of new technological advances (e.g. cloud deployment architectures) to ensure they are delivering the most efficient services.

CSI is often viewed as an ad hoc activity within IT services and is only triggered when IT management identify a problem. This is not the right way to address CSI. Often these reactionary events are not even providing continual improvement, but simply stopping a single failure from occurring again.

CSI needs a commitment from everyone in IT working throughout the service lifecycle. It requires ongoing attention, a well thought out plan, and consistent attention to monitoring, analysing and reporting results with an eye toward improvement.

Proper staffing and tools should be identified and implemented to support CSI activities.

6.3.1.5   Process activities, methods and techniques (CSI 3.9.3.1 ✔, CSI 4.1.5 ✘)

As its name suggests, and as illustrated in Figure 6.1, there are seven key steps in the seven-step improvement process.

While these seven steps appear to form a circular set of activities, in fact they constitute a knowledge spiral. Knowledge gathered and wisdom derived from the knowledge at one level of the organization becomes a data input to the next: from operational management, to tactical management, to strategic management.

Step 1 – Identify the strategy for improvement ✔

What are we trying to achieve for the business and how can the IT organization contribute through improvements? Take into account current and future plans.

Step 2 – Define what you will measure ✔

Compare what you should ideally measure with what you can actually measure, identify gaps, and develop a realistic measurement plan to support the improvement strategy. Take into account the current capabilities of tools and processes.

Step 3 – Gather the data ✔

Use monitoring to gather the data. Monitoring can be undertaken using technology and tools or can be a manual process.

Step 4 – Process the data ✔

Convert the data gathered into the required format for the intended audience. This can be seen as converting metrics into KPI results, and turning data into information.

Step 5 – Analyse the information and data ✔

Combine multiple sources of data and transform the information into knowledge. Develop an understanding of the real meaning of identified patterns and trends. Answer questions such as:

- Is this good or bad?
- Is this expected and in line with targets?

Step 6 – Present and use the information ✔

Communicate the information at the right level of detail for the audience and in a way that is understandable, provides value and supports informed decision making. Section 6.2.11 discusses reporting further and includes an example output.

Step 7 – Implement improvement ✔

Use the knowledge gained and combine it with previous experience to make informed decisions about the improvements that should be made. These improvements should focus on optimizing and correcting services, processes, tools etc.

6.3.1.6   Triggers, inputs, outputs and interfaces (CSI 4.1.6) ✘

Triggers

- Monitoring to identify improvement opportunities is and must be an ongoing process. New incentives may trigger additional measurement activity such as changing business requirements, poor performance with a process or spiralling costs.

Inputs

- Service catalogue
- Service level requirements (SLRs)

- The service review meeting
- Vision and mission statements
- Corporate, divisional and departmental goals and objectives
- Legislative requirements
- Governance requirements
- Budget cycle
- Customer satisfaction surveys
- The overall IT strategy
- Market expectations and competition
- New technology drivers (e.g. cloud-based delivery and external hosting)
- Flexible commercial models (e.g. low capital expenditure and high operational expenditure commercial models, and rental models).

Outputs

- Data required for metrics, KPIs and CSFs
- Service reports
- Improvement opportunities for inclusion in the CSI register
- Requests for change (RFCs) for implementing improvements.

Interfaces

In order to support improvement activities it is important to have CSI integrated within each lifecycle stage and within each process:

- **Service strategy**
  - Monitoring the progress of strategies, standards, policies and architectural decisions that have been made and implemented
  - Analysing results associated with implemented strategies, policies and standards.

- **Service design**
  - Monitoring and gathering data associated with creating and modifying services and service management processes
  - Defining what should be measured, KPIs and CSFs
  - Analysing results of design and project activities
  - Understanding trends when comparing results with design goals
  - Identifying improvement opportunities and analysing the effectiveness and ability to measure CSFs and KPIs defined when gathering business requirements.
- **Service transition**
  - Developing and testing monitoring procedures and criteria to be used during and after implementation
  - Monitoring and gathering data on the release of services and service management processes. Development of the monitoring procedures and criteria.
- **Service operation**
  - Monitoring of services in the live environment
  - Providing staff for monitoring and processing data, and analysing results as well as trends over a period of time
  - Identifying incremental and large-scale improvement opportunities.

6.3.1.7 Critical success factors and key performance indicators (CSI 4.1.12) ✗

Table 6.1 includes some sample CSFs for the seven-step improvement process. Each organization should identify appropriate CSFs based on its objectives for the process. Each sample CSF is followed by a typical KPI that supports the CSF. Each organization should develop KPIs that are appropriate for its level of maturity, its CSFs and its particular circumstances.

Achievement against KPIs should be monitored and used to identify opportunities for improvement, which should be logged in the CSI register for evaluation and possible implementation.

Table 6.1 Examples of critical success factors and key performance indicators for the seven-step improvement process

Critical success factor	Key performance indicator
All improvement opportunities identified	Percentage improvement in defects; for example, 3% reduction in failed changes; 10% reduction in security breaches
The cost of providing services is reduced	Percentage decrease in overall cost of service provision; for example, 2.5% reduction in the average cost of handling an incident; 5% reduction in the cost of processing a particular type of transaction
The required business outcomes from IT services are achieved	3% increase in customer satisfaction with the service desk; 2% increase in customer satisfaction with the warranty offered by the payroll service.

Note that because of the nature of the seven-step improvement process, it has to be applied to appropriate processes, activities, technology, organizational structure, people and partners for the benefits to be realized. This means that the KPIs used to judge the success of the seven-step improvement process are actually the KPIs from the other lifecycle stages and processes to which it has been applied. As a result the examples given here come from other areas.

6.3.1.8   Challenges and risks (CSI 4.1.13) ✗

Challenges

- Obtaining the required resources to implement and run the process
- Gathering the right level of data and having the tools to manipulate it
- Willingness of the organization to approach CSI in a consistent and structured way
- Obtaining sufficient information from the business regarding improvement requirements and cost reductions
- Persuading suppliers to include improvement in their contractual agreements; this is especially relevant for outsourced services.

Risks

- No formalized approach to CSI, initiatives undertaken in an ad hoc manner
- Insufficient monitoring and analysis to identify the areas of greatest need
- Staff attitude such as 'We have always done it this way and it has always been good enough'
- Inability to make the business case for improvement and therefore no funding for improvement initiatives
- Lack of ownership or loss of ownership
- Too much focus on IT improvements.

6.4   TECHNOLOGY CONSIDERATIONS (CSI 7) ✗

CSI activities require software tools to support the monitoring and reporting on IT services and to underpin the ITSM processes. These tools are used for data gathering, monitoring, analysis, reporting for services and assist in determining the efficiency and effectiveness of ITSM processes.

In a very small organization a simple in-house developed database system may be sufficient for logging and controlling incidents. However in large organizations, very sophisticated distributed and integrated service management tools may be required, linking all the processes with systems management toolsets. While tools can be important assets, in today's IT-dependent organizations, they are a means, not an end in themselves. When implementing service management processes, look at the way current processes work. Each organization's unique need for management information should always be its starting point. This will help define the specifications for the tools best suited to that organization.

Service management tools can be defined within broad categories that support and annotate different aspects of the systems and service management domains, including:

- ITSM suites and integrated toolsets, e.g. combined incident, problem and change management
- Knowledge management
- Configuration management system (CMS)
- Systems and network management
- Event management
- Automated incident/problem resolution
- Service catalogue management
- Performance management
- Business intelligence/reporting.

7 Competence and training ✔

Successful service delivery depends on personnel involved having the appropriate education, training, skills and experience. Specific skills, attributes and competencies are required by specific roles within ITIL service management.

There is also a set of generic attributes that are imperative for anyone carrying out any of the roles:

- Awareness of business priorities, objectives and drivers
- Awareness of the role IT plays in enabling the business
- Customer service skills
- Awareness of what IT can deliver
- The competence, knowledge and information necessary to complete the role
- The ability to use, understand and interpret best practice.

Standardizing job titles, functions, roles and responsibilities can simplify service management. The Skills Framework for the Information Age (SFIA) is an example of a common reference model for the identification of skills needed to develop effective IT services, information systems and technology.

Training in service management helps service providers build and maintain their service management capability. The official ITIL qualification scheme enables organizations to develop the competence of their personnel through approved training courses.

The scheme has four levels:

- Foundation
- Intermediate
- ITIL Expert
- ITIL Master.

There are also further complementary service management qualifications available which can contribute (accumulating credits) towards achievement of the ITIL Expert. Further details of these can be found at https://www.axelos.com/qualifications/itil/complementary-qualifications.aspx

7.1   FOUNDATION

The Foundation level ensures candidates gain knowledge of the ITIL terminology, structure and basic concepts, and comprehend the core principles of ITIL practices for service management. Foundation represents two credits towards the ITIL Expert.

7.2   INTERMEDIATE LEVEL

There are two streams in the Intermediate level, assessing an individual's ability to analyse and apply concepts of ITIL:

- ◼ Lifecycle stream
- ◼ Capability stream.

7.2.1   Lifecycle stream

Built around the five core publications for candidates wanting to gain knowledge within the service lifecycle context. Each module achieves three credits.

7.2.2   Capability stream

Built around four practitioner-based clusters for candidates wanting to gain knowledge around specific processes and roles. Each module achieves four credits:

- ◼ **Planning, protection and optimization** Including capacity, availability, continuity, security, demand and risk management

- **Service offerings and agreement** Including portfolio, service level, catalogue, demand, supplier and financial management
- **Release, control and validation** Including change, release and deployment, validation and testing, service asset and configuration, knowledge, request management and evaluation
- **Operational support and analysis** Including event, incident, request, problem, access, service desk, technical, IT operations and application management.

Candidates may take units from either of the streams to accumulate credits.

To complete the Intermediate level, the Managing Across the Lifecycle course (five credits) is required to bring together the full essence of a lifecycle approach to service management, consolidating knowledge gained across the qualifications scheme.

7.3   ITIL EXPERT

Candidates automatically qualify for an ITIL Expert certificate once they have achieved the prerequisite 22 credits from Foundation (mandatory initial unit) and Intermediate units (including Managing Across the Lifecycle, mandatory final unit). No further examination or courses are required.

7.4   ITIL MASTER

The ITIL Master qualification certificate validates the capability of the candidate to apply the principles, methods and techniques from ITIL in the workplace.

To achieve the ITIL Master qualification, the candidate must be able to explain and justify how they selected and individually applied a range of knowledge, principles, methods and techniques from ITIL and supporting management techniques, to achieve desired business outcomes in one or more practical assignments.

To be eligible for the ITIL Master qualification, candidates must have reached the ITIL Expert level and worked in IT service management (ITSM) for at least five years in leadership, managerial or higher-management advisory levels.

8 Related guidance

This section summarizes frameworks, best practices, standards, models and quality systems that complement ITIL practices.

8.1 ITIL GUIDANCE AND WEB SERVICES (SS APPENDIX D.1) ✗

ITIL is part of a portfolio of best-practice guidance, published by TSO. Further information, including the ITIL glossary, can be found at:

www.axelos.com

8.2 QUALITY MANAGEMENT SYSTEM (SS APPENDIX D.2) ✗

It's helpful to align service management processes with any quality management system already present in an organization. Total Quality Management (TQM) and IS9000:2005 are widely used, as is the Plan-Do-Check-Act (PDCA) cycle, often referred to as the Deming Cycle.

More information can be found at www.iso.org and www.deming.org

8.3 RISK MANAGEMENT (SS APPENDIX D.3) ✗

Every organization should implement some form of risk management, appropriate to its size and needs. Risk is usually defined as 'uncertainty of outcome', and can have both positive and negative effects. Management of Risk (M_o_R®),

ISO 31000, Risk IT and ISO/IEC 27001 all provide guidance related to risk management. See section 2.2.8 for further description of risk management.

8.4   GOVERNANCE OF IT (SS APPENDIX D.4) ✗

Governance defines the rules, policies and processes an organization needs to follow, and makes sure they are implemented consistently.

There are two ISO standards that relate to governance. ISO 9004 provides board and executive level guidance, and ISO/IEC 38500 provides for corporate governance.

8.5   COBIT (SS APPENDIX D.5) ✗

Control OBjectives for Information and related Technology (COBIT) is a governance and control framework for IT management. COBIT looks at what needs to be achieved, and ITIL provides complementary guidance about how to achieve it.

Further information can be found at www.isaca.org and www.itgi.org

8.6   ISO/IEC 20000 SERVICE MANAGEMENT SERIES (SS APPENDIX D.6) ✗

ISO/IEC 20000 is the standard for ITSM, applying to both internal and external service providers, although the standard is currently to be extended with the development of Parts 3 and 4:

■ ISO/IEC 20000-1:2011 Part 1: Specification (defines the requirements for service management)

- ISO/IEC 20000-2:2005 Part 2: Code of Practice (provides guidance and recommendations on how to meet the requirements in Part 1)
- ISO/IEC 20000-3:2007 Part 3: Scoping and applicability
- ISO/IEC 20000-4:2007 Part 4: Service management process reference model
- ISO/IEC 20000-5:2010 Part 5 : Exemplar implementation plan for ISO/IEC 20000-1
- BIP 0005: A manager's guide to service management
- BIP 0015: IT service management: self-assessment workbook (currently assesses against ITIL V2, to be revised via ITIL V3 complementary publications).

These documents provide a standard against which organizations can be assessed and certified with regard to the quality of their ITSM processes.

An ISO/IEC 20000 certification scheme was introduced in December 2005. A number of auditing organizations are accredited within the scheme to assess and certify organizations as compliant to the ISO/IEC 20000 standard and its content. The standard and ITIL are aligned, and ITIL best practices can help an organization looking to achieve ISO accreditation.

Further information can be found at www.iso.org or www.isoiec20000certification.com

8.7   ENVIRONMENTAL MANAGEMENT AND GREEN/ SUSTAINABLE IT (SS APPENDIX D.7) ✗

IT is a major user of energy, but can also support cultural and environmental changes as part of a green initiative. Green IT is about environmentally sustainable computing, from design through to disposal.

ISO 14001 is a series of standards related to an environment management system. Further details can be found at www.iso.org

8.8   ISO STANDARDS AND PUBLICATIONS FOR IT (SS APPENDIX D.8) ✗

There are many ISO standards and publications with relevance for IT and ITIL. Further details can be found at www.iso.org

Relevant examples include:

- ISO 9241: covers aspects that may affect the utility of a service
- ISO/IEC JTC1: deals with IT standards and publications
- The SC27 sub-committee develops ISO/IEC 27000, which relates to information security management (ISM)
- The SC7 sub-committee develops other relevant standards including ISO/IEC 20000 (service management), ISO/IEC 15504 (process assessment or SPICE) and ISO/IEC 19770 (software asset management).

8.9   ITIL AND THE OSI FRAMEWORK (SS APPENDIX D.9) ✗

The Open Systems Interconnection (OSI) framework was developed by ISO at the same time as ITIL V1 was written. IT practitioners may not realize common expressions like installation, moves, additions and changes (IMAC) are OSI terminology.

8.10 PROGRAMME AND PROJECT MANAGEMENT (SS APPENDIX D.10) ✗

Programme management can be used to deliver complex pieces of work, using interrelated projects. *Managing Successful Programmes* (MSP®) provides guidance related to programme management.

Portfolio, Programme and Project Offices (P3O®) provides guidance on managing these three areas together.

Project management guidance is found in *Managing Successful Projects with PRINCE2®* and the Project Management Body of Knowledge (PMBOK).

More information on MSP, P3O and PRINCE2 can be found at:

www.axelos.com

Further information on PMBOK can be found at:

www.pmi.org

8.11 ORGANIZATIONAL CHANGE (SS APPENDIX D.11) ✗

The organizational change aspects of IT change need to be considered to ensure that changes are successful. Kotter's eight steps for organizational change (www.johnkotter.com) are referenced in *ITIL Service Transition* and *ITIL Continual Service Improvement*.

8.12   SKILLS FRAMEWORK FOR THE INFORMATION AGE (SFIA) (SS APPENDIX D.12) ✗

SFIA provides a common framework for IT skills. This supports job standardization, skills audits and skills planning exercises.

SFIA is a two-dimensional matrix showing areas of work and levels of responsibility. Further information can be found at www.sfia-online.org

8.13   CARNEGIE MELLON: CMMI AND ESCM FRAMEWORKS (SS APPENDIX D.13) ✗

The Capability Maturity Model Integration (CMMI) is a process improvement approach applicable to projects, divisions or entire organizations.

The eSourcing Capability Model for Service Providers (eSCM-SP) is a framework to improve the relationship between IT service providers and customers.

SCAMPI assessments can be carried out against CMMI–Standard CMMI Appraisal Method for Process Improvement. More information can be found at www.sei.cmu.edu/cmmi

8.14   BALANCED SCORECARD (SS APPENDIX D.14) ✗

The balanced scorecard approach to strategic management was developed by Drs Robert Kaplan and David Norton. It views an organization from four perspectives to balance out the financial perspective which drives many decisions. The perspectives are:

■ Learning and growth
■ Business process
■ Customer
■ Financial.

The scorecard can be applied to IT quality performance and service operation performance. More information can be found at www.scorecardsupport.com

8.15   SIX SIGMA (SS APPENDIX D.15) ✗

Six Sigma is a data-driven process improvement approach. It identifies defects that lead to improvement opportunities. Six Sigma tries to reduce process variation. It has two primary sub-methodologies:

- DMAIC – define, measure, analyse, improve, control
- DMADV – define, measure, analyse, design, verify.

Further information can be found online, including Six Sigma overviews and training.

Further guidance and contact points

TSO

PO Box 29
Norwich NR3 1GN
United Kingdom
Tel: +44(0) 870 600 5522
Fax: +44(0) 870 600 5533
E-mail: customer.services@tso.co.uk
www.tso.co.uk

***it*SMF UK**

150 Wharfedale Road
Winnersh Triangle
Wokingham
Berkshire RG41 5RB
United Kingdom
Tel: +44(0) 118 918 6500
Fax: +44(0) 118 969 9749
E-mail: publications@itsmf.co.uk
www.itsmf.co.uk

BEST PRACTICE WITH ITIL

The ITIL publication portfolio consists of a unique library of titles that offer guidance on quality IT services and best practices. The ITIL 2011 lifecycle suite (five core publications) comprises:

- Cabinet Office (2011). *ITIL Service Strategy.* The Stationery Office, London.

- Cabinet Office (2011). *ITIL Service Design.* The Stationery Office, London.

- Cabinet Office (2011). *ITIL Service Transition.* The Stationery Office, London.

- Cabinet Office (2011). *ITIL Service Operation.* The Stationery Office, London.

- Cabinet Office (2011). *ITIL Continual Service Improvement.* The Stationery Office, London.

ABOUT *it*SMF

*it*SMF is the only truly independent and internationally recognized forum for IT service management professionals worldwide. This not-for-profit organization is a prominent player in the ongoing development and promotion of IT service management best practice, standards and qualifications, and has been since 1991. Globally, *it*SMF now boasts more than 6,000 member companies, blue-chip and public-sector alike, covering in excess of 70,000 individuals spread over 50+ international chapters.

Each chapter is a separate legal entity and is largely autonomous. *it*SMF International provides an overall steering and support function to existing and emerging chapters. It has its own website at:

www.itsmfi.org

The UK chapter has more than 8,000 members: it offers a flourishing annual conference, online bookstore, regular regional meetings, seminars and special interest groups and numerous other benefits for members. Its website is at:

www.itsmf.co.uk

ABOUT TSO

TSO is one of the largest publishers by volume in the UK, publishing more than 9,000 titles a year in print and digital formats for a wide range of clients. It has a long history in publishing best-practice guidance related to project, programme and IT service management – including ITIL and PRINCE2 – and is the official publisher for AXELOS. To accompany the core products, TSO also produces a range of complementary products to help users and organizations in their adoption of best practice. Details of all publications can be found at:

www.axelos.com